green
babycare

Susannah Marriott

LONDON, NEW YORK, MELBOURNE, MUNICH, and DELHI

Y'n gweras yma'n gorthyp
("In the soil lies the answer")

Project editor Tara Woolnough
Designer Hannah Moore
Project art editor Sara Kimmins
Senior editor Jo Godfrey-Wood
Photographer Tim Evan-Cook
Illustrator Anna Hymas
Managing editors Esther Ripley, Penny Warren
Managing art editor Marianne Markham
Jacket concept Sophia Tampakopoulos, Bryn Walls
Jacket designer Peggy Sadler
Production editor Ben Marcus
Production controller Wendy Penn
Creative technical support Sonia Charbonnier
Category publisher Peggy Vance

The suggestions in this book are not a substitute for qualified medical advice.
Always consult your doctor if you have any health concerns.

First published in Great Britain in 2008 by Dorling Kindersley Limited,
80 Strand, London WC2R 0RL. Penguin Group (UK)

2 4 6 8 10 9 7 5 3 1

A CIP catalogue record for this book is available from the British Library

ISBN: 978–1–4053–3112–8

Colour reproduced in Singapore by Colourscan
Printed and bound in Germany by Mohn Media

Mixed Sources
Product group from well-managed
forests and other controlled sources
www.fsc.org Cert no. SA-COC-1592
© 1996 Forest Stewardship Council
FSC

Discover more at
www.dk.com

Foreword

Birth signals the start of one of life's most special times, when everything seems possible. You will do anything and take on anyone to protect your baby.

If we can yoke this determination to do what's right for our children to this sense of unbridled power, we will surely be able to protect the future of the planet. Climate change is scary, but we have the means to make a difference because we hold the purse strings of the companies that are altering our environment by eating up natural resources, polluting the air, soil, and water, and emitting noxious gases. We buy the products and energy, and if we care enough, we can just stop doing so. We cared enough to make it impossible for GM foods to be grown for human consumption. We also cared enough to demand organic food, sales of which have grown tenfold in the UK in ten years. But how can an individual make a difference, faced with developing countries' rise in energy demand and governments unwilling to replace words with action? By making the world greener home by home and baby by baby, and creating a culture of change that can galvanize governments and manufacturers to take action. So hold your baby tight, feel the protective urge, feel empowered, then join together with others to demand change.

Susannah Marriott

Contents

INTRODUCTION

What actually is a "green" lifestyle, and
how could it make a difference for your family
and your baby, not to mention the planet?

The green agenda has become identified with climate change, carbon dioxide being its chief baddie (see pp9–11). But if we concentrate only on cutting carbon emissions, we miss the bigger green picture. This comes into focus only when we look at the kind of lifestyle that motivates our growing carbon emissions: shopping at out-of-town supermarkets with the same range of goods wherever we live; buying disposable high-street fashion that updates itself every five weeks; being so busy we drive places we could walk to; eating out-of-season produce from across the planet; accruing electronic goods; and keeping a home warm enough for vests all year-round. This life is unsustainable, whether underpinned by green or "brown" energy.

It's quite simple to be greener. Each of us – parents and babies alike – just needs to consume less. If we can do this, we also cut back on some of the man-made chemicals that sustain modern life (eg. in killing pests, making plastic bendy, preventing artificial objects from becoming a fire hazard) but which pollute the only things we really need: clean air, water, soil, food, bodies – and breast milk. Living green also means reconnecting to the places we live; by anchoring our lives in our local environment, from electricity to nappies, we create a truly green place to raise our babies.

THE HEALTH OF THE PLANET

The world's climate is changing. These are facts every parent needs to know, in order to understand why we need to act now to preserve the Earth.

The world's leading authority on climate change and its impact, the IPCC (Intergovernmental Panel on Climate Change), states that humans are responsible for most of the global-warming effect observed over the past 50 years, mainly by changing the Earth's atmospheric gases. A number of gases (known as greenhouse gases) cause the Earth to warm up: the most important is water vapour; the second, carbon dioxide (CO_2); others include methane, nitrous oxide, and ozone. Burning fossil fuels (oil, coal, and natural gas) and clearing forests are the primary human activities that have intensified this warming, since both release huge stores of carbon dioxide. What's the result? An increased likelihood of extreme weather, from torrential downpours and flooding, to heat-waves and "wildcat" fires; the warming of lakes, rivers, and seas; a shift in flora and fauna; and increased risk of species extinction.

Between 1970–2004,
CO_2 emissions increased by 80%

How might this affect the world our children will inherit? If it reduces agricultural land and biodiversity, and brings changes to the seasons and water availability, our ability to produce enough food will be seriously impaired. Heat-waves may trigger changes in the distribution of infectious diseases and greater mortality. Settlements in low-lying coastal regions or flood plains and mountains may be at risk. Social and economic instability, migration, and wars could follow.

Most European organisms and ecosystems will struggle to adapt to climate change

Greenhouse gas emissions rose by 70 per cent between 1970 and 2004, the largest increase coming from energy supplies, closely followed by transport. This trend is set to continue up to 2030, as developing countries increase their carbon dioxide emissions. But don't blame these countries; although it produces many of our consumer goods, the developing world's emissions are predicted to remain substantially lower than those of developed countries – in 1999 a mere eight nations were responsible for almost 50 per cent of carbon dioxide emissions globally: the US, Canada, Russia, Japan, the UK, Germany, France, and Italy.

The future of our babies is in our hands. It may be that we have only 12–15 years to stabilize greenhouse gases: after that we may not be able to halt the momentum. However, the IPCC agrees that modifying lifestyle and consumption patterns can reduce emissions. Using fewer resources has a positive effect, as do measures like managing transport and urban planning. Which way will we choose? We are the first generation to be able to take a lead, and pass on to our children the skills and technology to make life sustainable again.

Industrial consumption of natural resources and the consequent pollution have already radically altered our planet.

The basics of going green

"Reduce, reuse, and recycle" is the mantra of green parents; deep greens add in "refuse" and "repair". Notice where "recycle" comes in the list – if you do all the others, recycling tends to take care of itself.

The rules

• **Refuse** – you don't need most items touted in parent magazines. Chat to parents of older babies about what they could have done without. Don't accept plastic bags or excessive packaging. Above all, refuse fossil fuels by driving less, turning down the heating, and buying fewer air-freighted foods.

• **Reduce** – try three rather than five sleepsuits; walk, don't drive; and cut back on plastic toys (they waste oil, a precious resource that keeps carbon safely tucked away underground).

• **Reuse** – reusable bags are the easiest, but also try nappies, hardly worn clothes, and furniture from reclaimed timber.

• **Repair** – only allow into your home items that are built to last and that you'll want to repair and keep forever.

• **Recycle** – the last option when you can't fix something or pass it on; how little do you need to recycle?

Play the recycling game with your baby and it'll be second-nature by the time he's a toddler.

Introduction

A perfect time to change

A new baby often means rethinking every part of life: use this impetus to start living sustainably, and teach your child great green habits for life.

In the past 20 years, mankind's environmental footprint has increased dramatically with our snowballing use of natural resources, land, and energy. How you work and travel, where you live, what you eat, and when (or if) you sleep are all up for grabs after giving birth. Start making a difference with the resources consumed on your baby's behalf. This might seem crazy at a time when you're encouraged to consume more – to buy buggies, beds, and bottles – but your baby's future is a mighty motivator.

Simple green tips

• Do you need to fill the kettle to make up a feed? Boil only the amount of water you need. If we all did this, we'd save enough electricity to power most of the UK's street lighting.

• Are you doing more washing now? To reduce your impact on natural resources, replace detergent with eco-balls and hang nappies out to dry.

• Do you find you are using more tissues and loo roll to clean up? Choose recycled products; plant a tree or two; and join a campaigning environmental organization.

- Are you switching on the lights and heating more frequently now you're at home more? Change to a green energy tariff; insulate everything you can; turn off standby switches; and fight the urge to buy electronic baby items. The Energy Saving Trust estimates that by 2020, gadgets alone will account for 45 per cent of each UK household's electricity use – they currently make up about 33 per cent.
- Another mouth to feed? Choose seasonal produce from your region (more greenhouse gases are emitted flying in food than by the air-travel industry). When you eat meat, make sure it's locally sourced and ethically raised.

Before throwing something away, ask yourself where its ingredients came from and where they'll end up; are any hazardous for the environment? Could the item go somewhere else (for example, to a friend, or to the recycling plant), or could you have bought an alternative item with a longer life? If thinking this way causes you to buy less, your life will inevitably become more streamlined, even with a baby.

During 2004–2005, the amount of food air-freighted to the UK rose by 31%

Environmental impact, known as a carbon footprint, is measured in hectares

In the West, our **carbon footprint** is now 22 hectares per person. The **Earth's capacity** is just 16 hectares per person

Parental responsibilities

There's nothing like having a baby for making you more aware of your responsibilities, including not wrecking the planet for the next generation.

The human population has increased by one third since 1987. As the standard of global living conditions also rises, so does energy-related carbon dioxide emissions and pressure on basic resources such as water and land, as well as on biodiversity. So by creating more potential consumers of energy and resources, we parents are an important part of the problem! The Optimum Population Trust has even stated that the greatest thing anyone in Britain could do to help the future of the planet would be to have one less child.

As a first step, we can choose to consume less overall and more ethically, avoiding products created by companies whose actions harm the environment. Check out the environmental and ethical record of many companies at www.ethicalconsumer.org, which gives products an "ethiscore".

There is an abundance of ethical, organic goods now that more and more of us are going green: we might choose to chuck out our old mattresses, sofas, clothes, and cosmetics, and to ship in greener versions instead. But to be responsibly green, think minimal and local. Although this can seem an onerous responsibility, it's also a feel-good opportunity to teach children that material possessions don't really equal happiness.

Introduction

How green is your family?

Select the answers that best reflect the way you live now to find out how green your lifestyle is, and how you can become more eco-friendly.

HOME

1 Is your home well insulated?
A No; it's an old, draughty house.
B No, but we shut windows and doors, and draw the curtains at dusk to keep in heat.
C Yes; we have roof and cavity wall insulation and double glazing.

2 How green is your energy?
A Not at all; we leave appliances on standby all the time.
B We use energy-efficient lightbulbs and appliances.
C We have a green energy tariff.

3 Do you recycle?
A We're not very clear about what can be recycled.
B We recycle all we can via a kerbside collection.
C We compost and don't create much waste because we refuse, reuse, and repair things.

4 How do you save energy?
A By turning down the thermostat.
B We switch everything off at the sockets when not in use.
C We got rid of our TV and turn off lights if we're not in the room.

FAMILY FOOD

1 What do you usually eat?
A Ready-meals.
B Home-cooked dishes.
C Vegetarian home-cooked dishes.

2 Where do you buy most food?
A At the supermarket.
B From the local organic supermarket and health-food store.
C Directly from local suppliers.

3 Where do your organic fruit and vegetables come from?
A Abroad via the supermarket.
B A box scheme for local produce.
C We grow our own.

4 How do you carry your shopping?
A In plastic bags from the cashier.
B In heavy-duty reusable plastic bags.
C In Fairtrade cotton bags.

BABY FOOD

1 Where does your baby's milk come from?
A Regular formula.
B A combination of organic formula and breast milk.
C Breast milk.

2 If you're breastfeeding, what bodycare products do you use?
  A Whatever I find on the high street.
  B Certified organic products.
  C Nothing I wouldn't eat.

3 What are your baby's first foods?
  A Shop-bought purées.
  B Home-made organic purées.
  C Regular family food, mashed or cut into pieces.

4 What does your toddler eat?
  A Toddler ready-meals.
  B Mostly home-cooked organic children's food: fish fingers, pasta.
  C Whatever we're eating.

BABY CLOTHING

1 What does your baby usually wear next to his skin?
  A Sleepsuits from a multi-pack.
  B New organic cotton, hemp, or bamboo.
  C Cotton hand-me-downs.

2 Where are your baby clothes from?
  A Manufactured in the Far East.
  B Within the European Union.
  C Fairtrade projects.

3 What do you do with old clothes?
  A We throw them away.
  B Put them in with the recycling.
  C Hand them on to friends or charity.

4 How often do you wash baby clothes?
  A After each wear.
  B Just when they need a wash.
  C Only once we have enough for a full load, along with our regular washing.

BABY TOYS

1 What do you use as a teether?
  A A plastic teether.
  B An organic cotton teether.
  C A wooden teething ring.

2 What are your soft toys made of?
  A Synthetic fabrics.
  B Organic cotton, hemp, and bamboo.
  C Fairtraded organic fabrics stuffed with untreated wool.

3 Where do you buy toys?
  A From the high street.
  B From eco-friendly baby stores, catalogues, and websites.
  C From car boot sales, yard sales, charity shops, and online auctions.

4 Does your child have any battery-operated toys?
  A Yes; many.
  B Yes, but we only use recyclable batteries.
  C No, we prefer wooden or wind-up clockwork toys.

NAPPIES AND WIPES

1 Which type of nappies do you use?
  A Regular disposables.
  B Fully biodegradable disposables.
  C Reusable nappies.

2 How do you wash reusables?
  A At 60°C (140°F), with regular detergent and fabric conditioner.
  B At 60°C (140°F), with eco-detergent.
  C At 40°C (104°F), with eco-balls.

Introduction

3 Do you use baby wipes?

   A Yes, all the time.

   B Yes, but the organic type.

   C No; we make our own.

4 How do you deal with nappy rash?

   A With regular nappy-rash cream.

   B Certified organic barrier cream.

   C We use homeopathic creams.

CLEANING

1 What do you wash clothes with?

   A Regular detergent.

   B Eco-detergent.

   C Eco-balls or soap nuts.

2 How do you dry clothes?

   A In a drier than turns itself off when clothes are dry.

   B At the launderette.

   C We mostly line dry.

3 How do you clean surfaces?

   A With bleach-based cream cleaners.

   B With an eco-spray.

   C With lemon juice or vinegar.

4 How do you clean carpets?

   A Steam cleaning.

   B A sprinkling of bicarbonate of soda and vacuum cleaner.

   C We don't have carpets.

BABY'S ROOM

1 Where does your baby sleep?

   A In a brand-new cot.

   B On an organic cot mattress.

   C With us.

2 How is the room furnished?

   A From the high street.

   B With second-hand furniture.

   C With furniture we already had around the home.

3 What DIY materials do you use?

   A Regular paint from the DIY store.

   B Low or no-VOC paints.

   C Nursery-grade eco-paints and bamboo wallpaper.

4 What bodycare products do you use on your baby?

   A High-street baby products.

   B Certified organic baby products.

   C Olive oil and Castile soap.

COMMUNITY

1 Who do you socialize with now you have a baby?

   A We mostly stay at home and stay in touch with people online.

   B We trek across town on the bus to meet up with old friends.

   C We've found many new friends via a local baby-massage group.

2 Where do you hang out?

   A At friends' homes.

   B In a local baby-friendly organic café.

   C At baby reading/play sessions at the local library.

3 Do you use a nursery?

   A We travel to a recommended playgroup.

   B We walk to a local playgroup.

   C We set up a local playgroup ourselves.

4 Do you use your local park?
   A We use a better one a ride away.
   B Yes; we've become quite friendly
   with the local teenagers.
   C Yes; we joined a committee to raise
   money for better facilities.

TRAVEL

1 How do you get to work/school?
   A In our car.
   B On the bus or train.
   C We walk or cycle.

2 Where do you take holidays?
   A Wherever we choose.
   B At an eco-destination abroad.
   C Within this country (by train).

3 What type of fuel does your car use?
   A Diesel.
   B Biodiesel or electricity.
   C What car?

4 How do you get around locally?
   A We drive everywhere.
   B I have a baby seat on the bike.
   C We pop the baby in the buggy and
   walk most places.

ANSWERS

Mostly As

You're not very green yet, but
are taking some tentative steps
to changing the way you live for
the better. Can you change your
life a little further now by
thinking a little more deeply
about some of your lifestyle
choices? Try adopting some B
and C answers in the future.

Mostly Bs

You're making a good effort at
leading a greener life. Perhaps
there are a few more simple
steps to take you a little further?
Could you cut back on buying
brand-new items (even if they
are organic), walk more places,
and try to reuse things more?

Mostly Cs

You're many times greener than
the average family in the UK,
and so you're making a
difference already. Keep up the
good work! Who can you pass
this book on to once you've
finished with it? And what else
could you do to become "deep
green"? Could you add a layer of
sheep's wool insulation to your
loft, or even consider generating
your own green energy at home?

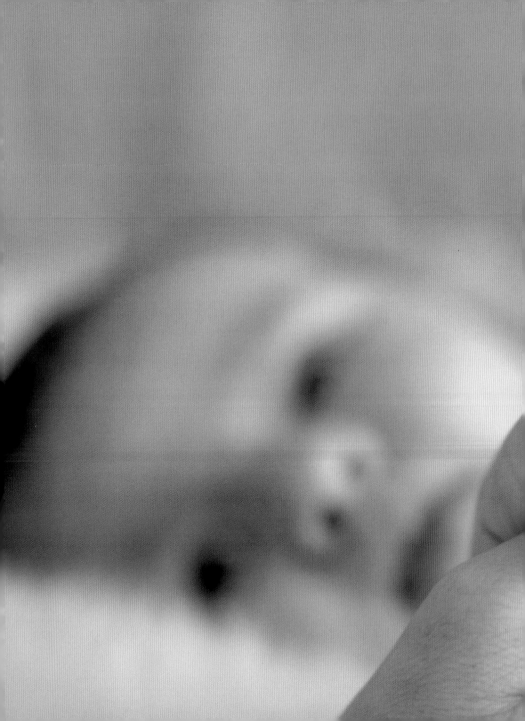

Caring for your new baby: starting green living from day one

Green health

A greener approach to health means taking
a more holistic view of yourself and your baby,
and preventing illness before it occurs.

Holistic health involves recognizing that we are part of an
ecosystem, and that whatever we put into the environment
comes back to us via what we eat, drink, breathe, and absorb
through skin; your baby will start to absorb toxins through the
placenta while still in the womb. So, caring for the good health
of the environment directly benefits us as well. A balanced
lifestyle, including a nutritious diet, regular exercise (after your
six-week check-up), and a positive attitude, will help keep you
and your family happy and in good health.

REST AND RECUPERATION

Aim for two weeks' "lying in" time to sleep, boost your
strength and milk supply by eating healthy meals, and
to gather your inner resources for the months to come.

It is important to rest adequately after giving birth; this aids
recovery, and allows you to bond with your new baby. If you're
lucky enough to have a support network ask for assistance where
you need it, as most people are only too happy to help. At first,
you may want to minimize the number of visitors you have, as

they can be extremely tiring. When you do receive guests, you might ask for help with small jobs. Being beholden to others makes it more likely you'll help them in the future, and this forges the close-knit communities that engender green living.

How to ensure good rest

- Set aside a fixed period of postpartum rest, to smooth the transition into motherhood and avoid ill health.
- Climb into a freshly made bed in soft organic cotton pyjamas that open down the front for easy breastfeeding.
- Doze when your baby sleeps, rather than trying to get back to your "normal" life.
- Lie skin-to-skin with your baby every day and sing to her; this type of bonding leads to easier breastfeeding and sleeping.
- Spend time gazing into your baby's eyes when she wakes.
- Stop, close your eyes, and allow your breath to become slower and deeper. This relaxed focus will help calm you.
- Ask for a home treatment from a therapist who specializes in postnatal massage, if friends offer to treat you.

Rest is a seriously undervalued healer in our super-speedy culture

BABY MASSAGE

Massage is the perfect way to increase confidence in handling tiny limbs, to soothe an unsettled baby, and to promote sleep and development. Choose a time between feeds when your baby is content. You don't need oil for this massage, which is performed over clothes.

1 Sit with your back well supported and knees raised, thighs together. Place your baby tummy-down on your thighs, head turned to one side. Using the back of your right fingers, lightly stroke from your baby's right hip to right shoulder. Now using your left hand, repeat on her left side. Alternate several times to create a seamless flow of strokes.

2 Taking one foot in your cupped palms, use your thumbs to stroke from toe to heel. Repeat on her other foot.

3 Turn your baby over. With two fingers, trace a square from her right hip to rib cage, across the abdomen, down to the left hip, and back to the start. Build up an even, flowing movement.

4 Take each hand in your palms, and make circles around your baby's palm with your thumbs. Feel them relax as you circle. Talk or sing to your baby as you work.

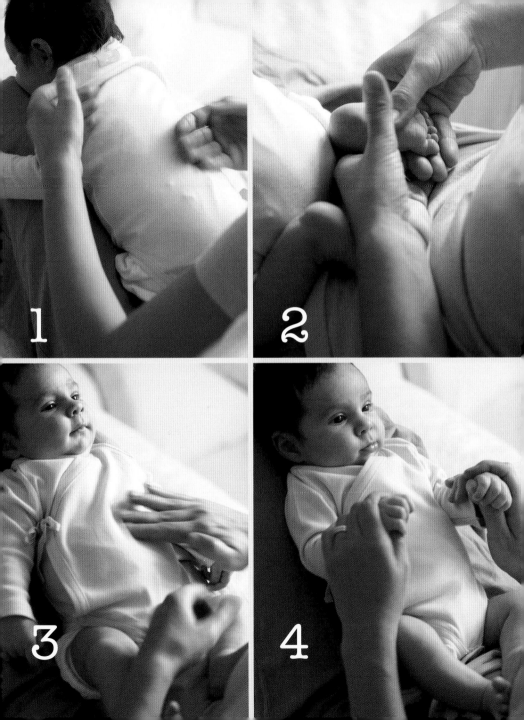

GREEN HEALTH & BODYCARE FOR NEW MUMS

Now you are a mum, it is important to try to reduce the number of man-made chemicals you apply to your own skin, as well as your baby's, as these may be transferred to your baby via your milk if you are breastfeeding.

Skin absorbs 60 per cent of what's applied to it – 80 per cent if it's wet. Rub-in (as opposed to rinse-off) products are of particular concern, since it's tricky to find cosmetics and bodycare products that don't contain one or more of the following: hormone-disrupting parabens; phthalates toxic to the reproductive system; irritants from artificial fragrance; genotoxic formaldehyde; the pesticide triclosan; or by-products of oil refining. Surprisingly, many products named "organic" or "natural" still contain synthetic chemicals. To be certain products are free from these, choose only those with Soil Association, Demeter, BDIH, Ecocert, or ACO logos.

Replace regular sanitary towels (which contain plastic, bleached wood pulp, pesticide residues, and GM products) with organic disposables, and discard them with household waste – four million are flushed every day in the UK and the plastic liner lasts indefinitely. To reduce landfill waste and manufacturing processes, try washable Fair Trade hemp or organic cotton pads (soak in cold water after use, then machine-wash). Once you start having periods again, consider a reusable silicone menstrual cup, which functions on a principle similar to the contraceptive cap. For tissues and toilet paper, choose unbleached 100 per cent post-consumer recycled; this takes 30–50 per cent less energy to produce than paper from trees, and cuts pollution into the atmosphere by an incredible 95 per cent.

Natural remedies for new mums

- To ease rough skin, rub in cold-pressed hemp oil, which contains the perfect balance of omega-3 and omega-6 fats.
- For shock after birth, take Bach Flower Rescue Remedy or Australian Bush Flower Essences Fringed Violet.
- To build up your milk supply, take homeopathic remedy *Dulcamara 30* three times a day for a few days; drink plenty of nettle and fennel tea.
- For engorged breasts/mastitis, take *Belladonna 30* as often as needed until symptoms improve.
- To relieve painful or cracked nipples, take *Phytolacca 30* three times daily, and apply calendula cream between feeds.
- For inflamed breasts, take the central rib out of two Savoy cabbage leaves, bruise gently, and place inside bra cups.
- For cuts, tears, and bruises, take *Arnica 30* and *Calendula 30* alternately every 2 hours for a few days. If you have a surgical wound or were given an epidural, take *Hypericum 30* as well. Add 3 drops of calendula tincture either to your sanitary pad or into a bath, for its gentle healing properties.

GREEN HEALTH CARE FOR BABIES

Increasing numbers of parents are choosing to combine complementary therapies with conventional medicine to treat minor ailments in the first few months of life and throughout childhood.

A kit of health-care essentials from the herbal and homeopathic pharmocopoeia can help tackle the most common childhood illnesses and minor first aid. However, if your baby has a fever, breathing problems, extreme vomiting, or diarrhoea, call a doctor at once.

Every green bathroom cabinet should include a homeopathic first-aid kit. Available from homeopathic pharmacies and health-food stores, these include around 35 remedies for common complaints with a booklet explaining how to use them. To give homeopathic remedies to a young baby, dissolve one pill in a teaspoon of boiled water and spoon into her mouth once cooled. Also make sure you have calendula cream, Bach Flower Rescue Remedy, and essential oils of lavender, tea tree (for their anti-microbial properties), and myrtle (a decongestant).

Alternative medicine is popular with parents because it tends to be gentle and have few side effects

When required, place 1–2 drops of essential oil in an electric vaporizer while you bath your baby (but be careful not to leave this on for too long – under 1 hour is fine).

Natural remedies for babies

• For a jaundiced baby, breastfeed frequently and if the weather is fine, take her outside to get some sunshine (wrap her up warmly). A few doses of the homeopathic remedy *Chelidonium 30* can be enough to resolve most mild cases.

• For persistent dry, flaky skin, massage your baby with avocado oil (which is rich in vitamin E), or pour a cup of camomile tea into a morning or evening bath.

• To ease colic caused by intestinal gas, give your baby *Colocynthis 30*, especially if she pulls her legs up to her chest while crying. If a baby stretches out or arches her back when upset, the best remedy is *Dioscorea 30*.

• For nappy rash, apply calendula cream after every change and leave your baby nappy-free as often as you can. *Sulphur 30* soothes red, raw nappy rash caused by acidic stools.

• To relieve painful teething, gently rub homeopathic chamomilla teething granules into your baby's gums with your finger until the granules dissolve.

• To promote sleep or ease crying, add 2 drops of Rescue Remedy to 30ml (1fl oz) of cooled boiled water and rub 4 drops of the mixture behind the baby's ears.

Caring for your new baby: Green health

Your **natural immunity** can be seriously **compromised** by factors such as **stress,** a high-**sugar** diet, and frequent use of **antibiotics**

IMMUNIZATION

Whether or not to have your baby vaccinated may be the first major dilemma you face as a parent. It is interesting that policies vary widely across the globe, with certain vaccinations mandatory in some countries but not used at all in others.

The first step is to become an informed parent by researching the various immunizations using reputable sources and reading through the sites of vaccine-awareness groups online (see p185). Do discuss with your doctor concerns you might have regarding links between vaccination and allergies, and the much disputed association with autism. You might enquire about production and the additional ingredients (apart from the vaccine itself), such as antibiotics, formaldehyde, and mercury. Ask about common side effects and the latest research on safety, as well as why some parents avoid vaccination or pay for separate jabs.

Conventional medicine holds that when all the risks from childhood illnesses are taken into consideration, a child is better off being immunized. You should also consider the health of your community, and the risk to other babies and children if you decide against vaccination: more than 92 per cent of the population must be immune to a virus to prevent an epidemic. If you opt out of vaccination, it can help to join a support group of like-minded local parents, who may throw chickenpox or mumps parties so that children catch the diseases in childhood and gain immunity.

Caring for your new baby: Green health

Green baby clothing

Shopping for baby clothes is irresistible, but young babies don't need many items at a time. By buying second-hand, you can keep virgin materials where they belong: on trees and in the ground.

In their first year, babies consume a staggering number of clothes, growing out of garments in three months or less (thankfully, this slows in the second year and beyond). The plus side is that this has given rise to second-hand baby shops, online auctions, and Freecycle sites crammed with beautiful, inexpensive baby clothes, and friends with slightly older babies keen to pass on hardly worn goodies.

For a minimal layette, try four to six bodies and sleepsuits (look for nickel-free poppers), two draw-string sleeping gowns, two to three pairs of trousers or dresses, three cardigans, a hat and mittens, and four to six pairs of socks and/or tights. Buy bigger than you think (start with three- to six-month rather than newborn size) and forget shoes till your child starts walking. It's likely you'll be given more stuff than you need. Take some back to exchange for more durable items such as an organic lambskin, or items she will grow into later.

Eco-options for baby clothes include hand knits (top), bamboo shirts (bottom right), and second-hand clothes

CHOOSING THE GREENEST FIBRES

A brand-new white cotton sleepsuit – what could be purer for a new baby's delicate skin? Well, quite a lot. Unfortunately, brand-new white cotton is far from pure and further from green.

Cotton doesn't grow well without water, chemical fertilizers, herbicides, defoliants, and pesticides – it uses around 25 per cent of the world's insecticides and 11 per cent of all pesticides. These pollute the soil, water sources, and marine environment (so also our tap water and the fish we eat), and traces may remain in the finished fabric. Cotton workers (and their babies) are exposed to known carcinogens and developmental toxins. White cotton fabric may be chlorine-bleached, which releases dangerous dioxins into the atmosphere, while coloured cotton may contain dyes known to be hazardous to health or skin-sensitizing. And cotton grown in America, Australia, India, or China may be genetically modified, the risks of which are indeterminate; yet, paradoxically, GM cotton can reduce the impact of pesticides.

One solution is to choose organic cotton. For cotton to be certified organic, it cannot be grown with synthetic chemicals, nor mixed with regular cotton, so it may both feel softer and be of better quality as a result. Look for the Swedish KRAV stamp of approval (Europe's oldest and most prestigious badge of organic production, which guarantees social rights for the producers).

Hemp is the eco-fabric of choice for baby clothes. One of the world's fastest-growing crops (it can be harvested after just 100 days), it produces double the amount of fibre per acre as cotton with little need of insecticides, herbicides, or water, and almost all of the plant can be used. A new crop is sown directly after harvesting, for constant renewal of soil carbon, and it leaves the soil weed-free and detoxed of excess nitrogen, preventing pollution of water sources. Because hemp fibres are longer than cotton fibres, the fabric is incredibly durable, and clothes tend to keep their shape despite wear and washing. Favour hemp grown in the UK and Europe.

Bamboo fabric feels like silk against precious baby skin and becomes softer with washing, making it ideal for pass-on clothing. Like hemp, it requires minimal pesticides, fertilizers, and water to grow; indeed, it's so hardy that it suits land prone to drought or flooding and combats soil erosion, helping communities in areas affected by climate change. Bamboo grows quickly (harvested every two to five years), takes up little space, and both pumps more oxygen into the atmosphere and traps atmospheric carbon dioxide more effectively than most trees. It absorbs dye easily, reducing the need for chemicals and huge amounts of water. Bear in mind that much of the crop is grown in and transported from the Far East.

Eco clothing solutions

It's not just eco-fabrics that count; being a green parent means thinking about how garments have been made and transported, how durable they are, and the lives of the people who made them.

Be aware of dyes and finishes; if a garment isn't certified organic, it may have been treated with up to 250 heavy metals and synthetic chemicals for easy care, to prevent shrinkage, and to add flame retardance or colour. These include hormone disruptors, skin irritants, and carcinogens, which may persist in the environmment and pass into our bodies. Avoid any garment with a "new car" smell. Stick to creamy unbleached fabrics in the early days or those dyed with "low-impact" vegetable or clay dyes.

"Clothes miles" encompass more than the distance from warehouse to shop. Manufacturers – even organic ones – might buy raw materials in one country, then send them across the world for spinning, weaving, or making up before shipping back. Favour companies that grow, spin, sew, and sell in one place.

Choose second-hand first. Look for organic cotton or hemp and indulge your label lust sometimes – designer labels create incredibly well-made clothes with smooth seams that pass on better than cheap sweat-shop garments. When you buy new, look at a company's ethical trading policy: does it pay a fair price for materials and labour, source locally, and minimize its packaging?

light green Buy new Fairtrade unbleached organic cotton garments – the fabric itself contains no traces of harmful chemicals that might irritate your baby's especially sensitive young skin, and growing and manufacturing involves very few chemicals. Buying Fairtrade also has a positive impact on the farmers who grew the cotton crop (and their families).

 **mid green** Use second-hand garments passed on from another baby. Look for hemp, a wonder eco-fabric with incredibly durable fibres that keep their shape after washing better than almost any other fabric, giving the garment many potential lives. These garments become softer with wear and are also naturally resistant to harmful UV rays. Remember to pass on to another baby afterwards.

deep green Knit your own bootees, hat, or cardigan from unbleached pure new wool from a local farm (look for the words "untreated" or "pure grow"). The benefits include cancelling out air miles, championing local farmers and heritage breeds, and cutting out garment-manufacture processes – plus your baby gets a bespoke garment that you'll want to keep for your next baby or pass on to someone else.

Washing baby clothes

For such tiny creatures, babies generate a crazy amount of washing. To make sure that your laundering is green as well as clean, take care when selecting your washing-machine (and drier, if you need one), and adopt sensible laundry habits.

Many parents upgrade their washing-machines to coincide with a new baby, but what's the greenest choice now that most new machines have the EU's "A" or "A+" energy label? Consider the

whole life of the machine and its repairability; more expensive manufacturers tend to produce reasonably priced parts that make repairs economical. Budget suppliers may not do this, making machines cheaper to replace than repair. Also think about where the machine was made. Those with an EU Eco-label are made with fewer flame retardants and hormone-disrupting chemicals. A second-hand machine may be another option, but ensure it is energy-efficient.

Line drying baby clothes preserves their lifespan, and reduces your use of energy-consuming tumble-driers.

Green laundry solutions

The amount of energy we use in washing and drying clothes forms a large (and growing) part of the resources a home consumes – more than 8 per cent of electricity and 14 per cent of water.

Reducing water temperature is the easiest way to greener laundering since up to 90 per cent of the electricity used is to heat the water. Wash most loads at 40°C (104°F), or even 30°C (86°F); use cold water for woollens and delicates, and reserve 60°C (140°F) for heavily soiled items.

Greener, plant-based detergents, unlike regular petroleum-derived washing powders, are made from renewable ingredients that decompose, causing less water pollution. And because they don't contain whiteners, brighteners, or enzymes that attach to clothing, they are less likely to cause skin irritation. Use half to a quarter of the recommended amount, as a baby's skin is five times thinner than an adult's; if your baby has especially sensitive skin, try none at all. Avoid softener altogether; its skin-irritant ingredients stick to fabric and transfer to baby skin. Eco-balls and soap nuts are probably the best option, as they require no detergent, softener, or rinse cycle.

Among the least energy-efficient of appliances are tumble-driers (though launderette ones are far better); line drying is the greenest option, and is less likely to shrink or damage fibres.

light green Put on a full load: each wash uses about as much water as a bath – around 80 litres (21 gallons). Doing fuller loads less often not only preserves water and energy, but extends the lifespan of your washing-machine. If you use a tumble-drier, clean the filters as recommended, to increase efficiency. Don't forget to switch your electricity supply to a sustainable source.

mid green Washing a full load at 40°C (104°F) rather than 60°C (140°F) cuts electricity use and carbon emissions by one-third. Use only eco-friendly detergents, and cut back on the amount you use, or try none at all; petroleum-derived fragrances from laundry were detected in 27 per cent of streams studied in a US survey – they can irritate delicate new skin and respiratory systems.

deep green Clothes soiled with baby sick or worse obviously need a wash. But if garments are only lightly soiled, fold them to wear again and start using bibs. Another plus of not washing is clothes that look newer for longer. Real wool and silk garments always need less washing. Washing-machine use is up by 23 per cent in 15 years, from an average three to four loads a week – see if you can cut back to one or two.

Feeding your baby:
the healthiest foods for you, your baby, and the planet

You are what you eat

Humans are at the top of the food chain: grass absorbs nutrients from the soil; a cow eats the grass; we drink its milk. And when your baby drinks your milk, he jumps to the top of the chain.

What's the problem? Put simply, it's that much of our food may be contaminated with low levels of man-made agricultural and industrial chemicals. Some, such as pesticides and growth promoters, may be sprayed on to or injected into crops and livestock; others have leached into the soil through decades of fertilizer and pesticide use, or have been pumped from industrial plants into the atmosphere or rivers, then carried out to sea and absorbed by marine life. Other synthetic chemicals are transferred to food from plastic packaging. Some of the most dangerous chemicals for humans, such as dioxins from chlorine bleaching and PVC manufacturing, persist in the environment indefinitely, since there's nothing to neutralize them.

Many of these environmental toxins seem to get stored remarkably well in the very foodstuffs we need for a healthy diet: oily fish, milk, fruit, and vegetables. After we consume them, the fat-soluble chemicals amass in our bodies over a lifetime – especially in women's bodies, which are naturally fattier than men's – and the only surefire way to detox is if you starve. If you get pregnant or breastfeed, then the toxins pass on to your baby.

A 1999 WWF report detected more than 350 synthetic chemicals in breast milk. They included PCBs (found in meat, fish, and dairy food) and alkylphenols (in ready-meal packaging) that have the potential to interfere with natural hormone balance, even in very low doses, and may affect the development of the brain and the reproductive and immune systems. Some researchers posit a link with the rise in allergies, autism, behavioural problems, obesity, and early puberty. But no tests have actually been carried out on the safety of multiple exposures to cocktails of industrial chemicals for adults, let alone infants.

Fortunately, there's something positive we can do. Firstly, eat certified organic foods, which are grown without pesticides or many of the man-made chemicals used to raise conventional crops and livestock. Secondly, avoid processed foods, which tend to contain artificial additives and be swathed in plastic packaging. Instead, choose fresh, seasonal, local produce; this usually results in reduced carbon emissions, too.

Greenpeace estimates that your **body** may contain up to **200 synthetic chemicals**

Feeding your baby: You are what you eat

EATING ORGANIC

About half of the fresh foods tested in the UK annually contain traces of pesticides. It's easy to avoid them: just eat organic whenever you can.

Organic farmers are permitted to use only minimal artificial chemical fertilizers and pesticides, animals are reared without routine drugs, antibiotics, or growth hormones, and organic certification guarantees food is free from genetically modified material. Organic food-processing standards strictly govern what additives can be added to processed foods. The Soil Association, for example, permits only 29 of 500 licensed EU additives.

Recent studies suggest that organic foods are higher in nutrients than conventionally farmed produce, with greater amounts of vitamins, minerals, and antioxidants. UK research found, for example, that organic spinach, cabbage, potatoes, and lettuce have a hugely increased mineral content over conventional crops (up to 100 per cent more in spinach), and organic tomatoes have almost double the antioxidant flavonoids. American studies reported 58 per cent more antioxidants in organic fruit, along with double the calcium, four times the magnesium, and 13 times the selenium in organically grown wheat. Organic milk has superstar status, with 68 per cent more omega-3 fatty acids than regular milk, plus more vitamins. Free-range organic chicken was found to have 25 per cent less fat, and far more flavour.

Feeding your baby: You are what you eat

By nurturing the health of the soil, raising a mixture of crops, and valuing sustainability, organic farming seems to promote good water quality and biodiversity – studies by Natural England (formerly English Nature) and the RSPB show that organic farms shelter more birds, butterflies, and bats than conventional farms. They also provide one-third more local jobs. The organic Rodale Institute in the US claims that organic farming can significantly reduce emissions of climate-changing gases by conserving more carbon in the soil than regular farming practices, which can deplete carbon content by up to 75 per cent.

In a UK poll, more than 70% of consumers reported that organic fruit, vegetables, and meat taste better

Consumer demand is now bringing more UK organic produce than ever into supermarkets. Look for the Soil Association logo, which guarantees the world's most stringent environmental and animal-welfare standards. Or the Demeter symbol of biodynamic farming, which takes organic principles further, raising plants to the cycle of the moon and planets, treating soil with homeopathic remedies, and setting the needs of workers and community at the centre of its holistic vision.

Organic must-haves

- **Dairy foods** – fat-soluble toxins accumulate in fatty foods, so make milk, butter, cheese, and yogurt an organic priority.
- **Meat** – organic meat is free from routine antibiotics and growth-promoting hormones, and sausages are made with fewer additives. Stock grazed on pasture, not processed feed, may contain more omega-3 fatty acids (and better flavour).
- **Fruit** – in 2003, all citrus fruit tested in the UK contained pesticide residues, most from multiple sources. Organic fruit isn't waxed or dosed with fungicides after harvesting.
- **Salad leaves** – lettuces are sprayed with more pesticides than any other crop. Pillow packs are chlorine-rinsed, and modified-atmosphere packaging can destroy nutrients.
- **Oily fish** – wild salmon and organically farmed salmon and trout contain fewer gender-bending PCBs.
- **Sugary foods** – sugar-beet is one of the most heavily sprayed of conventionally farmed crops and provides half the sugar used in the UK; sugar-cane production is very polluting and highly damaging to biodiversity.
- **Bread** – organic loaves are free from flour- and dough-improving artificial chemicals and bleaching agents.
- **Wholegrains** – conventionally farmed whole grains store a whole dose of pesticides.

Shop locally for organic produce, and take a reusable shopping bag with you.

LABELS AND PACKAGING

Learn how to read and interpret the information on a label, and it becomes surprisingly easy to rid your family diet of many potentially harmful ingredients in food and its packaging. Vote with your purse by boycotting the items below.

Ingredients to avoid

• **Soya** – found in 60 per cent of processed foods and in "vegetable" oil, soya may be genetically modified but is not marked as such. Soya is transported over 5,000 miles (8,000km) to the UK to make feed for intensively reared livestock. Farming soya has cleared thousands of square miles of Amazon forest, and led to rural migration.

• **Sweeteners** – in the US, saccharin (E954) is graded as an "anticipated carcinogen"; aspartame (E951) can be neuro-toxic; high fructose corn syrup has been linked to diabetes.

• **Trans-fats** – (labelled "partially hydrogenated" fats) common in processed foods, these have no nutritional value and are associated with disorders such as coronary heart disease.

• **Synthetic dyes** – a 2007 study linked these food colourings to hyperactivity in children when mixed with the preservative sodium benzoate (E211): E110, E122, E102, E124, and to a lesser extent, E129.

• **Preservatives** – the following have all been associated with health risks: E320–1, E250–2, E220–1, E223–4, E621.

Try to avoid buying food that is packaged – even in biodegradable options, as these only fully degrade when industrially composted (such systems are rare in the UK). Plastic packaging, from clingfilm to plastic bottles and microwavable ready-meal trays, is especially harmful to the environment and human health. When PVC (labelled with a "3" in a triangle) is manufactured or destroyed, it pumps dioxins into the atmosphere – exposure can cause human reproductive, developmental, and neurological problems. It also releases heavy metals such as mercury; it is estimated that 1 in 6 newborn babies in the US have levels of mercury high enough to cause brain damage and impair language and co-ordination skills. The plasticizers (phthalates), which make plastic flexible, can be transferred to foods, especially "wet" products (those containing fat). We can inhale them, or they can leach when packaging is heated at high temperatures and they can scramble normal hormone function. Cans may contain bisphenol-A, an oestrogenic chemical that affects the reproductive system in even small doses. Glass and unbleached paper are greener choices.

An Italian study showed that 88% of newborn babies tested positive for plasticizers in their bodies

Eating local

Eating seasonal local food can be a better option for the health of your baby, your family, and the whole planet than eating organic.

When you eat fresh foods produced locally, you reduce food miles: the distance your dinner travels from all the places it was raised, processed, and packaged to reach your plate. This cuts down on the climate-change emissions caused by transporting food by plane, ship, and lorry, and by the refrigeration needed to keep it fresh in transit. It may also decrease the number of post-harvest chemicals used to keep produce from spoiling. Fresh ingredients are less likely to be processed or over-packaged, saving the carbon emitted by cooking and chilling, as well as the unrecyclable plastics that usually head straight to a landfill site.

All these factors can make local food greener than organic food. Though more organic produce is now sourced nearer home, the burgeoning popularity of organic food in the UK means that much still has to be imported from around the world.

Buying local produce also supports your local community: not only small family farms, but the independent shops on the high street that stock their produce, from greengrocers, and bakers, to the butchers and fishmongers fast being put out of business by our love of buying packaged produce all in one place.

With the decline of such independent shops, we lose a wealth of knowledge about where food comes from and when, and how to prepare and cook it. Supporting local producers also helps to keep their small, local suppliers in business – window cleaners, builders, cafés – which ensures a thriving high street for all. If it motivates you, think of buying locally as a form of local Fairtrade that keeps wealth, services, and even schools in your community.

You're also more likely to be tempted by seasonal food: displays of produce and prices in local stores may vary from month to month, unlike well-stocked supermarkets. Natural therapists extol the health benefits of eating seasonally; not only do ripe, just-picked ingredients retain nutrients lost in storage, but because our bodies are adapted to the seasons, we feel better by eating lighter foods in summer and heartier fare in winter.

Why avoid supermarkets? They tend to knock down prices for suppliers; their demand for perfectly shaped produce renders delicious but nobbly apples and carrots worthless, and their centralized distribution increases food miles.

In a German study, it took
5,000 food miles
to bring together the ingredients for
strawberry yogurt

Every £10 you spend in a local shop invests £25 in your community

But for every £10 spent in a supermarket only an extra £4 stays in your community

BUYING LOCAL PRODUCE

Buying local produce at bustling farmers' markets, delis, and farm shops makes a very stimulating day out when you have young children.

Support your local farmers' market. Babies in buggies love a lively street market and it's a great place to meet growers and find out how their crops were cultivated and livestock reared. Plan an afternoon outing to a pick-your-own field or farm shop with tea rooms or a pets' corner; look out for toddler arts projects linked in with seasonal produce, such as pumpkin days in the autumn. Visit your local butcher; he'll be able to tell you which farms your meat came from. Eating less meat is one of the greenest things you can do, since intensive meat production consumes so much water and fossil fuels, and directly causes huge emissions of methane and slurry, the UK's biggest source of water pollution. Treat meat as a *treat*: take all the money you'd spend on factory-farmed meat at the supermarket and turn it into one high-quality item from a small producer, or try a cheaper cut for slow cooking. While you're out, this is the place to find the ultimate free-range food: rabbit and game.

In the early days of motherhood, home delivery is the best eco-shopping choice: have a milkman deliver returnable, toxin-free glass bottles and get a weekly organic fruit and vegetable box. You could even set yourself a challenge to see if you can source everything you eat from within 50 miles.

Feeding your baby: Eating local

Growing your own

The most local food is the food you grow in your own backyard – and you don't need acres to do this. A few pots and window-boxes can yield a surprising amount of produce, from potatoes to exotic berries.

More and more families are keen to trace their food from garden fork to dinner fork: in 2007, vegetable seeds outsold flower seeds for the first time in the UK since the Second World War, and demand for allotments is at an all-time high. You might quake at the thought of giving yourself any extra work, but growing in pots is relatively hassle-free (no digging and little weeding). And if you buy young plants, you cut out the worry about whether seeds will germinate (though toddlers love that bit). Involve your baby in planting and watering; let her get muddy. If you can't deal with soil, sprout seeds in a jar – toddlers relish the juicy crunch of sprouted chick-peas.

Easy crops children love to grow
- Tumbling cherry tomatoes in hanging baskets.
- Blueberry bushes in pots of ericaceous soil, or soil-planted apple trees native to your region.
- Lettuces and spring onions in a window-box.

As well as learning about the seasons and how food grows, children exposed to soil may be less prone to allergies.

- Basil raised from seed on a window-sill.
- Alfalfa sprouts in a sprouting vessel such as a jar.
- Potatoes or garlic in half barrels, or carrots in large pots (an effective natural barrier to carrot-root fly).

Cooking at home

Home-cooking is the greenest habit we can cultivate, as it allows us to choose the best ingredients, ditch unnecessary packaging, and pass on invaluable skills.

The essence of good home-cooking is really great ingredients: butter instead of low-fat spread; fresh egg custard, not custard powder. When ingredients are fresh, ripe, and pure (read local, in season, and unprocessed), they are full of natural flavour and need only minimal cooking – saving fuel and retaining maximum nutrients. In the UK, we eat 40 per cent of all the ready meals sold in Europe; yet with simply a tasty loaf, some ripe home-grown tomatoes, and a chunk of regional cheese, you have lunch. Add a salad, a whizzed-up soup, and a plate of seasonal berries with local cream or yogurt: now you have a feast.

Cooking from scratch involves knowing what's best when – when are oysters in season, when can you pick damsons? It's also about the art of conjuring up delicious dishes from left-overs. The average household in the UK bins a third of its food; most goes directly to landfill sites. Lastly, don't leave the microwave on standby: it uses more energy for the clock than in cooking.

Engage your toddler when preparing food, so she learns the pleasures of home-cooking early.

Eco shopping solutions

Food and drink production is thought to be responsible for about a third of a family's environmental impact. The Fairtrade movement says we can change the world by shopping selectively; use the power in your purse to start reducing the impact your family makes.

To avoid endangered fish species, favour those with the Marine Conservation Society's logo. Its website lists which products are available where (see p186). Also try to avoid long-line and trawler-caught pelagic fish – trawling in particular causes the death of dolphins, turtles, and other marine mammals. Line-caught by hand is the best choice.

The way people in your region have eaten for centuries has moulded the landscape: the livestock raised and crops grown determine the look of fields and hedges. To preserve the countryside, buy traditional foods that support small farms. If we don't, farms may turn into second homes, fields become golfcourses or scrubland, and communities start to falter.

To change the world further afield, try some Fairtrade fruit, sugar, coffee, tea, and cocoa. Fairtrade companies bring ethically raised food to a world market, helping to bring employment and prosperity to farmers and their regions. Fair terms are agreed for products, and environmental standards are often good.

light green Buy organic foods from a supermarket, choosing locally grown produce over imported goods. Reject packs flown in from abroad (air-freighting has a much greater environmental impact than transportation by sea or road). Select food with little or no packaging, and check that what packaging there is can be completely recycled. Or leave it behind at the checkout.

mid green Shop at your local high street and farmers' market to cut your number of trips to out-of-town supermarkets – we drive an average 135 miles (217km) each year to shop for food. Again, favour locally produced goods (food miles rose by 15 per cent between 1992 and 2002) and foods with less packaging. Always take along fabric bags or baskets to carry your shopping in.

deep green Grow some of your own food, raid the hedgerows, and swap with friends. Supplement with a box delivery from a local organic farm. A vegetarian meal cooked from all-local ingredients has top eco-credentials, a 2003 Swedish study found, equating to around just 190g (6½oz) carbon dioxide release; a meaty meal made of mostly imported ingredients increased the carbon load to 18kg (4lb).

Breastfeeding

Breastfeeding couldn't be more environmentally beneficial; it means no food miles, no packaging, no need for washing or detergents, no reliance on formula powders made by multinational conglomerates, no electricity-guzzling fridge or sterilizer – for six whole months or more.

What's not to like? Well, it can hurt at first, be hard to master without expert help, and confine you to hours on the sofa and wakeful nights. Breastfed babies tend to wake more often through the night, feed more frequently during the day, and can take less readily to scheduled feeds than bottle-fed babies.

But consider the superlative health benefits for mother and baby. Breast milk provides the perfect mix of nutrients, as well as protection against infections and environmental contaminants. From the first feed onwards, breastfed babies benefit. They tend to be more intelligent, healthier, and more resistant to infections, allergies, diabetes, and obesity. Even if only breastfed for one month, their health is improved up to age 14, compared with babies who have not been breastfed at all.

Breastfeeding deepens the bond between mother and baby as well as providing long-term health benefits for both.

Breastfeeding mothers also reduce their own risk of osteoporosis and cancer of the breast and ovaries, and get back in shape more quickly after the birth. Most mothers who give up breastfeeding say they would have liked to have kept it up for longer, but lacked support. The best help comes in person; day or night, call your hospital's breastfeeding counsellor. If you're out of hospital, call a breastfeeding helpline (see p186) – staffed by trained, experienced breastfeeding mothers. Or, you might drop in on a breastfeeding coffee morning (held at local cafés or community centres), where other mothers can reassure you. Alongside the confidence that comes with expert advice, the key to success in breastfeeding consists of perseverence, patience, and willpower.

It's helpful to know that your baby's "weird" feeding habits are completely normal

There are considerable advantages to breastfeeding beyond weaning. Even when solid food is providing your baby's main nourishment, breast milk continues to confer immunity from germs (in studies, breastfed toddlers get ill less often than other children). It is also a lovely way for your child to feel safe and nurtured when she's venturing out into the world. If your only feeds are before bed and first thing in the morning, each day begins and ends in a loving, green way, and you may even be able to bypass bottles altogether.

EXPRESSING MILK

Want to breastfeed and still have a life? Try expressing some milk. This way, dads also get a chance to nurture their baby with nature's most renewable resource.

Allow a few weeks to establish breastfeeding before you attempt expressing milk. To find out how to express by hand (the greenest way), ask a breastfeeding expert or look online (see p186). However, many mothers prefer to use a hand-held pump, which gently draws the milk into an attached bottle. Another reason to express is to build your milk supply: pump after feeding, and in a few days you'll make enough milk for your baby, plus extra to freeze. Expressing also relieves aching breasts of over-abundant milk. But don't feel discouraged if you can't express (some of us just can't) or if your baby refuses a bottle; he may accept it from someone else.

Breastfeeding kit

- **Breastfeeding bra** – buy at least two (get them fitted by a professional) and try out the organic options.
- **Breast-pads** – washable silk, wool, bamboo, or hemp feel softer against delicate skin than paper disposables.
- **Expressing machines** – borrow first to see which you get on with: speedy hospital-style pumps or hand pumps.
- **Storage jars** – use lidded glass bottles; more immunity properties are preserved by refrigerating than by freezing.

SUPERFOODS FOR BREASTFEEDING

Superfoods are those that are considered especially nutritious or beneficial to health. By eating the right foods when breastfeeding, you can keep yourself fit, build a healthy supply of milk, and protect the planet, too.

You need around 300–400 extra calories a day for the first three months of exclusive breastfeeding. To ensure you are eating a balanced diet, these calories should come from a variety of foodstuffs; if you select local and seasonal produce, which varies your diet as different items come into season, you will effortlessly achieve a good mix of nutrients.

Left to right: calcium-rich yogurt also contains healthy bacteria; lemons (unwaxed) provide vitamins C and A; Swiss chard is high in vitamins and minerals; red peppers contain antioxidants; oily fish boasts essential omega-3 fatty acids; and oats are a good source of soluble fibre as well as a range of vitamins.

Essential foods

- **Fruit and vegetables** – aim for more than five a day, including some green leafy vegetables and orange, red, or yellow produce. Organic food means far fewer pesticide residues, and as fruit and vegetables are the largest category of air-freighted goods, you should try to choose local and seasonal produce. However, do note it can be greener to import foods that grow easily abroad (eg. tomatoes, citrus fruit) than to grow them in northern climates in artificially heated glasshouses.
- **Oily fish** – eat about twice a week, choosing fish that harbour fewer toxins, such as sardines and herring.
- **Whole grains** – seek out organic loaves with no soya flour, enjoy organic oats for breakfast, and try grains like spelt.
- **Dairy produce** – organic is free from hormones; natural yogurt has more calcium than milk.

Eating **conventionally farmed** foods means that your **breast milk** could contain higher levels of **dioxins** than those permitted in pasteurized **cow's milk**

AVOIDING TOXINS

The idea of banned toxins in breast milk is frightening. Do you need to worry? And what can you do to green your life and detox your chemical load?

All breast milk contains measurable levels of industrial chemical contaminants, wherever you live and whatever your lifestyle. This is because fat stores toxins very well, making naturally fatty breast milk an important indicator of the levels of contaminants in our food chain. These contaminants leach out of paints and industrial detergents, from pesticides and PVC plastic, and seep into our bodies via our skin and through the stuff we eat from high up in the food chain. So the toxins in breast milk merely reflect the general level of environmental pollution. This does not mean that you should stop breastfeeding, which boosts immunity and thus helps limit damage from environmental pollutants. What you *can* do is campaign for more research into the effects of man-made toxins. Join the WWF, write to your MP, or start a blog. We can only clean up the environment by getting together and acting globally. Take some practical measures to minimize your direct toxin intake, too. Eat organic foods and use safe bodycare products (see p28); spend less time close to electronic equipment and plastic; avoid large oily fish with mercury residue (stick to herring and sardines); and decorate with eco-paints. Above all, stop smoking and make your home a smoke-free zone.

Holistic bottle-feeding

An advantage of bottle-feeding is that dads, grandparents, and other carers can also bond with your baby, whether using expressed breast milk or formula milk.

There are various reasons why some women are unable to breastfeed; and even those who do may decide it is just not practical all the time. The easiest way to make bottle-feeding a more personal experience is by ensuring some skin-to-skin contact as you nestle together, to promote intimacy and stimulate your baby's sense of smell and touch.

The man-made toxins found in breast milk have been well publicized, but that is not to say that formula milks have any less of a toxic load. In fact, as most formula is made from cow's milk, it will be prone to the same type of contaminants. You may add more into the mix from tap water, formula containers, and the actual bottle, even if the ingredients of the powder are all organic. The cultivation, processing, and packaging of formula milk may also shed carbon dioxide and toxins into the environment; fossil fuels are burned in manufacture, transportation, and refrigeration, forests are cleared for cattle-grazing, and packaging is bleached and printed on.

Very few babies are born with lactose intolerance, but even if your baby is, try to avoid soya-based formula. Intensive

Always make up a fresh bottle of formula milk for each
feed, and consider using a water filter for tap water.

cultivation of the crop in Brazil has resulted in the destruction of
pristine rainforest and widespread rural unemployment. Soya
accounts for the highest percentage of pesticide sales worldwide,
and much of the crop is genetically modified (even when not

labelled as such); no trials have been done on the safety of GM material for infants. Soya milk also contains plant oestrogens, which certain studies have shown can affect the development of a baby's reproductive system and the brain. Goat's milk formula is no longer recommended as an alternative, as it still contains some lactose. Speak to your GP about selecting an appropriate formula for your baby.

For the bottle itself, strengthened glass bottles are the greenest choice (see p186). Most baby bottles (95 per cent) are made from polycarbonate plastic (marked with a "7" in a triangle). This contains bisphenol-A, an oestrogen-mimicking chemical that can have adverse effects on development at even very low doses; it may leach into milk when the bottles are heated or scratched. A better plastic is polypropylene (marked with a "5"). It's one of the plastics with the lowest impact on the environment, and it doesn't contain any bisphenol-A.

By 4–10 weeks, **75%** **of mothers** either **use infant formula** entirely or alongside breastfeeding

STERILIZING

All bottle-feeding equipment should be sterilized for your baby's first year, as milk can get encrusted in the grooves and become a breeding-ground for bacteria. However, if you start weaning your baby at six months, you won't need to sterilize bowls and spoons.

Rather than accumulate more new electrical equipment, see if you can borrow a steam-sterilizer from another mother who is not currently using hers. Or, look for a steamer or bottles you can put directly into the microwave, the most energy-efficient form of heating. To avoid extra equipment altogether, set aside a large pan and boil items in it for ten minutes (though this destroys teats very quickly). Using the dishwasher is not the greenest option: it has to run at 80°C (176°F) to sterilize. You can sterilize in completely cold water, but this requires tablets that leave an after-taste. Solar kettles have been an important development for sterilizing water in developing countries.

Immunity-boosting tips
- Breastfeed for as long as possible, if you are able.
- Sterilize bottles but don't be too neurotic about cleanliness; your baby needs exposure to germs to develop immunity.
- Avoid antibiotics unless absolutely necessary.
- Consult a homeopath about treatments that will strengthen your baby's constitution.

Feeding your baby: Holistic bottle-feeding

Green weaning

Babies need nothing other than milk for the first six months of life. Then things get interesting (but more messy) as you introduce them to the world of good eco-food.

You'll know when your baby is ready for something more than milk by the way she watches you eating and mimicks chewing or reaches out for food. Don't be tempted to start your baby on solid food before the age of six months (talk to your doctor or health visitor if you have concerns or if your baby was born prematurely): babies weaned after six months are less likely to develop food allergies.

Try to make your baby's first tastes organic. Researchers from the University of Washington found that children who ate organic food had six times less pesticide residue in their bodies than those fed on non-organic foods. The standards for tolerable levels of pesticides on foods are based on what's considered safe for adults. No research has been done to determine safety for infants, nor any tests into the effects of long-term exposure to low-level cocktails of chemicals. Babies may be more at risk, not just because the brain and immune system are vulnerable during development, but because babies eat more in proportion to their size, and an immature digestive system absorbs toxins effectively but undeveloped organs aren't able to eliminate them very readily.

The Environmental Working Group states that the greatest pesticide risk comes from just 12 foods

The traditional way to start weaning is to offer a little rice cereal mixed to a sloppy consistency with your baby's regular milk. Don't force it: babies get all the nutrients they need from milk up to the age of one. When your baby is happily eating baby rice, you can gradually add puréed fruit and vegetables and other grains one by one, waiting a few days to check for reactions before adding a new food. After eight months, try some protein-rich foods, such as organic chicken or lamb, lentils, eggs, cheese, and yogurt.

That said, many parents are now choosing to ignore the guidance on purées (developed when we started weaning at three or four months, when babies can't hold up their heads nor manipulate well from hand to mouth). Instead, they offer finger foods: bite-sized chunks of food that the baby feeds herself. This is known as baby-led weaning. Whichever approach you choose, offer cooked vegetables (especially) and fruit before you start your baby on proteins, and make sure to buy organic when it comes to the pesticide "dirty dozen": peaches, apples, bell peppers, celery, nectarines, strawberries, cherries, lettuce, grapes, pears, spinach, and potatoes.

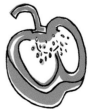

Feeding your baby: Green weaning

SUPERGREEN FINGER FOODS

Babies weaned directly on to finger foods are less likely to be fussy eaters, say advocates of this method, because they learn to cope with the texture and taste of real food from the outset.

Giving finger foods is certainly less stressful than lovingly preparing a purée only to watch it being spat out and smeared over the table. Start by offering your baby foods cut into fist- or chip-sized shapes for easy grasping. You could try steamed broccoli, carrots, or new potatoes, green beans or asparagus, some roast squash, pasta shapes, or a hunk of "real" bread (supermarket bread made by the industrial Chorleywood method is too pappy, unless toasted), perhaps smeared with hummus or avocado. Sit at the table as your baby gums and sucks the food in case he gags (a safety reflex to prevent choking). Indeed, the reason baby-led weaning seems to be so effective is that your baby eats alongside you – and the same food as you – from day one, rather than getting fixated on sweet, bland purées. Your baby also takes control, choosing what to eat and how much; which means you lose some control. This method of weaning is messier than offering neat spoonfuls of purée, and wiping the mouth after each one, but have courage!

Start your baby on finger foods, and he's more likely to become an adventurous eater.

Feeding your baby: Green weaning

MAKING FIRST PURÉES

When you make your own baby food from
fresh fruit or vegetables, you can reassure
yourself about their provenance: for this method, you
could use apples, carrots, squash, or other produce.
Use a hand-powered mouli, which requires no electricity
and allows you to vary the texture for your growing baby.

1 Wash the produce very well, scrubbing with a brush
reserved for this. Peel all non-organic orchard fruit and
root vegetables. Remove the stones or core the fruit.

2 Steam the vegetables or fruit for a few minutes until
quite soft but not falling apart. Or you could simmer in
a scant amount of water instead.

3 Grind the vegetables or fruit with the hand-powered
mouli until you have a purée with a consistency
appropriate for your baby's age.

4 Spoon enough for one meal into your baby's bowl,
adding milk or cooking water if necessary. Store the
remainder in the refrigerator in clean, lidded glass jars for
up to two days, or freeze immediately in a non-plastic ice-
cube tray (label with the date and use within six months).

Eco baby food solutions

Baby food is now the single largest sector of the organic market. Since 2004, more than half the jars of baby food on the shelves have been certified organic, which is very reassuring. But which are the greenest options for feeding your baby?

Not all organic baby food is the same. Before you buy, make sure to read the label, checking the ingredients list and the sell-by date. There's a world of difference between jars of food that were processed from cheap and bulky root vegetables and lots of water before you even got pregnant, and freshly made food with quality ingredients with real flavour. In this case, the ultimate test of quality is the taste test. Buy a few different pots and have them for lunch. If you wouldn't eat the food yourself, why give it to your baby, who has many times the number of taste buds you have? If you can afford it, always choose baby foods with the shortest shelf life (some stay fresh for just days). However, if you have the option, cooking your baby's food yourself is the greenest and tastiest course of action, whether you opt for purées and reusable storage jars or think outside the jar and head straight to finger foods. Cooking with seasonal ingredients not only helps the environment, but it also ensures that your baby meets an ever-changing variety of foods, lessening the risk of over-exposure to pesticide residues from any single ingredient.

light green Buy pots of organic food from the supermarket. The greenest choices probably won't have been heat-processed, and so you're more likely to find them in the chill cabinet or freezer; these are most likely to taste like "real" food. Or, better yet, if you shop at a nearby farm or organic supermarket, you might even come across a range made locally – it will taste better, too.

 **mid green** Make your own baby food from local, seasonal organic ingredients. This saves food miles and the fossil fuels spent in industrial production processes. Feeding your baby seasonal foods has health benefits, too: Austrian research shows that produce picked in season is higher in nutrients (especially vitamin C, which degrades in transit) than flown-in ingredients.

deep green Ditch special baby foods and give your child the home-cooked food you eat (with less salt), dining together as a family as often as you can. Change your recipes with the seasons or according to what arrives in your weekly organic vegetable box. Show your baby how good home-cooked dishes taste (whether organic or not) and you are setting him up to eat well for life.

Eating as a family

Before your baby celebrates his first birthday you have a window of opportunity to influence his eating habits for life. Will he prefer processed tastes or be prepared to try anything?

If everyone in your household sits at a table together, your baby will recognize the sociable, bonding properties of eating long before he smears his first fistful over his face. Even if you can't eat as a family

all the time, you can still turn off the TV (a great green habit); sit at a table; lay the table with cutlery (with a set for your baby too); not have anything else on the table (no books or toys); and decide when the meal ends. It may be easier to allow finger foods in front of the TV, but it's a habit your child may still be in by his early teens. Cut out processed food, and above all, eat together and eat the same food so you don't lead two food lives – now that's green.

Making mealtimes calm periods when you share time as well as food leads to more adventurous eaters and less food in the bin.

GREEN MEALTIME EQUIPMENT

Mealtimes with a baby at the table mean a little more equipment is required. Here are the green items to prioritize, from high chairs to sippy cups.

Bibs are essential if you're not to add to your wash load. There are Fairtrade organic cotton versions, or you could try tying an old-fashioned adult pinny around the baby's neck (to cover him to his toes); pick them up at charity shops. Some babies like a hard pelican-style bib they can retrieve fallen food from (hard plastic contains fewer plasticizing chemicals than flexible plastic).

Plastic bowls are never good for the environment – their manufacture and incineration sheds toxins into the environment that endanger human health. Some campaigners worry that plasticizing chemicals in plastic baby bowls might leach into food, especially when a bowl is scratched. Don't heat up food in plastic either: decant it into a heat-proof container instead. You might like to try a Fairtrade bamboo baby bowl and cutlery set or a stainless steel bowl, which will last forever. As your baby gets older, he might even graduate to ceramic bowls (in the plural; don't get too attached to any one, as there are likely to be breakages). If you're worried about potential toxins in plastic sippy cups, choose a safer one made from a plastic other than polycarbonate (so avoid those marked with a "7" in a triangle). Or, you could search online for stainless steel versions (which also don't taint the drink with a plastic taste, and are very resilient).

You might not need a high chair when you start giving your baby his first taste of solid food – he'll be happy to sit on your lap to begin with – but as soon as he can sit unsupported, he'll enjoy having his own space at the table (even if the food doesn't stay there). The world's best-selling children's chair, the wooden Stokke Trip Trap, is probably the greenest there is because it "grows" with your baby; you can adjust it to bring him to the perfect level for eating at an adult table as a baby, toddler, preschooler, school-child, and even as a teenager or adult. And it's a design classic that will still look good at a table when your children have left home. Baby chairs that clip to the side of the table use fewer raw materials than a full-size chair, are portable, and also ensure that your baby eats at a table like you, not at a plastic tray (though do be prepared for food to slide about, making some mess on the table). Avoid chairs with vinyl, padding, and frilly bits that just get food-infested – chairs you can hose down with a shower-jet are best for ease of cleaning.

It's a good idea to put something under the high chair to catch at least some of the mess. If you don't want plastic in your green home, use recyclable newspaper or a square of eco-friendly linoleum (made with linseed oil and jute, it's completely biodegradable).

The green, clean baby: gentler approaches to washing and cleaning

What is clean?

US studies suggest that the air inside homes can be many times more polluted than outdoor air, even in cities. This has much to do with the chemical cocktail of cleaning products we use.

80% of most people's exposure to **pesticides** occurs when they are **indoors**

Most cleaning products available in supermarkets are chock-full of ingredients that aren't good for the environment or your baby. Most non-eco cleaners contain petroleum-derived surfactants (detergents), such as SLS, that don't readily biodegrade or may form dangerous compounds as they do so. They may also contain hormone-disrupting phthalates, phosphates, musks, or colourings (none of which has to be detailed on the label). The effects of polluted indoor air are worst for those who spend most of their time indoors, and the very young. Living in an over-clean home in the first year of life is also associated with a heightened risk of allergies and asthma. Epidemiologists say that our high standards of cleanliness (and small family size) mean that babies are less exposed to germs now than in the past, with the result that their under-used immune systems may then over-respond to common substances such as pollen and dust. Chemicals in cleaning products have also been linked to asthma. Don't throw the dodgy ones in the bin (straight into landfill) or down the drain (into the water supply); see if your waste collection service accepts hazardous chemicals, or call a local Friends of the Earth group for advice (see p185).

What to chuck out

• **Cleaning fluids** – (even eco ones) containing glycol ethers, terpenes, or limonenes (in pine or citrus scents); a 2006 report said they create toxic air conditions in confined space.

• **Air fresheners** – young babies exposed to air fresheners have been found to be prone to diarrhoea and ear infections.

• **Chlorinated ingredients** – look for the term "chlor-" in heavy-duty products such as bleaches. The manufacturing process is deadly and chlorine reacts with organic material to create compounds hazardous to the environment.

• **Anti-pest products** – whether for home, garden, or pets, they are likely to contain pesticides (*cide* means killer).

• **Anti-microbials** – don't clean better than soap and water, and are banned in some hospitals because it is feared they lead to superbugs. They can contain up to 275 pesticides, and traces have been found in breast milk and fish.

• **Aerosols** – blast neuro- and reproductive toxins and respiratory irritants directly into the respiratory tract.

Greener home cleaning

There are many effective green cleaning products you can buy – but you might find the most eco-friendly already on your own kitchen shelves.

When there's a baby in the house, shop for green cleaning products that suit people sensitive to dyes and fragrances. Buy products at a place where you can refill them, or choose concentrates in smaller bottles; the largest component in household cleaners is water – that's a lot of carbon dioxide expended on transporting coloured water. You might like to enquire about the manufacturer's animal-testing policy (some claim that to make products greener, they have to use newer ingredients that need to be animal-tested).

Be aware of the air in a room when you're cleaning, especially if your baby is with you: his respiratory system is immature, and humidity increases the chances of irritant ingredients penetrating his respiratory tract. Avoid products that spray into the air; be sure to rinse very well; and throw open windows, especially if your home is green and well insulated, keeping them open for a few hours, until the smell disappears. Store used cleaning cloths well out of the way of inquisitive hands. Also pay attention to the floor – the place where babies spend a large part of their first couple of years, when their brain, internal organs, and immune system are developing. Any products sprayed indoors eventually settle on the floor, as do toxins tramped in from outdoors on shoes. These then mingle with dust from computers and other electronic equipment that may be laced with flame-retardant chemicals which have been linked to reproductive and neurological disorders.

Consider ridding your home of carpets. The largest dust reservoir in a home, a typical carpet contains high levels of heavy metals such as lead, pesticides, PCBs (linked with impaired cognitive abilities in infants), and PAHs (from car exhausts and smoking, and associated with DNA damage).

Children playing or crawling on carpets may ingest 5 times more dust than adults

If your carpets are providing important insulation to your home, just bear in mind that 25 sweeps with a powerful vacuum cleaner are needed every week for a few weeks to detox a carpet. One of the easiest ways to reduce the toxins and dirt entering your home is to instigate a no-shoes policy. Fit a deep doormat and leave indoor shoes or slippers by the door.

The green, clean baby: Greener home cleaning

Green cleaners

- **White vinegar** – dilute with water to make a wipe for surfaces, glass, and tiles, or use neat to unclog showers and sinks. The vinegar smell disappears as it evaporates.
- **Lemon juice** – squeeze neat on to surfaces and chopping boards to de-grease and for a bleaching effect.
- **Salt** – use for washing-up or to scour baked-on pans.
- **Spices** – simmer a handful of dry spices (try cinnamon sticks, cloves, fresh ginger root, cardamom seeds, star anise), or slices of lemon, lime, and orange, to scent your home.
- **Bicarbonate of soda** – mix into a paste for sinks and tubs, or sprinkle into the toilet bowl, add white vinegar, and scrub.
- **Microfibre miracle cloths** – just dampen and rub. These need no solvents or detergents to get rid of grease and stubborn stains. Wash in the washing-machine when dirty.
- **Wet-dusting solution** – mop with liquid Castile soap, then rinse with water plus 10 drops of essential oil of grapefruit.
- **Raise a plant** – many broad-leaved house plants neutralize airborne toxins like formaldehyde and benzene.
- **Shake and vac** – sprinkle bicarbonate of soda over carpet, leave for a couple of hours, then vacuum.
- **Loo-seat spray** – add 10 drops of anti-bacterial tea tree essential oil to water in a mister, shake, then spritz.

Encourage your young child to help with household chores so that she feels she is a valued member of the family cleaning team.

Washing your baby

Babies don't need a bath every day until they start crawling (when they can get filthy quickly). In the early days, save water and protect your baby's skin by simply topping and tailing daily.

Topping and tailing is an easy and eco-friendly way to keep your baby clean (see pp98–99), and cuts down on the number of baths your baby needs until she starts getting properly dirty with the onset of solid food and crawling. At least until this point, no baby needs commercial cleansing products: yes, that really does mean no soap, baby bubbles, shampoo, lotions, or oils. Many cleansers – or even too much tap water – can irritate or damage a baby's delicate skin. The barrier layer of skin is immature during the first year of life and absorbs water more readily than mature skin, making it vulnerable to irritants and water-soluble toxins in skincare products. It also loses moisture more quickly, so the fewer drying detergents the better. Plain warm water is usually enough to get rid of most mess, and organic olive oil makes a good wipe for stuck-on stuff and is emollient for dry skin. As a

An infant's skin does not develop a barrier to environmental toxins for 2–3 years

last resort, use a small amount of organic baby soap. Some parents like to use natural sponges, which are gentle on the skin, biodegradable, and compostable.

A slippery baby and unconfident parent make a scary combination, while plastic baby baths can be cold and hard for a baby (as well as non-sustainable). Many green parents find sharing a bath with their baby is a more bonding, friendly, and secure experience (it saves water too). Bathing together can soothe an agitated baby and help to lift parental exhaustion in the evening. Keep the water tepid (around 38°C, 100.4°F) and don't add any oils or bubbles. Turning down the thermostat on your water heater to 49°C (120°F) earns you extra eco-points.

Get into the bath, then have someone pass you the baby. Cuddle your baby in the water at first, keeping her body and shoulders submerged, but resting on you until you both feel more relaxed. Then swim her through the water, with her head and neck firmly supported. When your baby is able to sit up, sit her opposite you in waist-high water and sink down so that your faces are at the same level; this makes a great opportunity to talk to each other. Ask your baby a question and see how she answers with splashes. When you've finished a bath, pass your child to an adult waiting with a warmed hooded towel to dry and dress her in warmed clothes while you climb out. Babies lose body heat very quickly. Never leave your baby or toddler unattended in or near a bath, or even turn your back on her for a moment.

TOPPING AND TAILING

Cleaning your baby's face, hands, and bottom is all that's needed in the early weeks and protects her new skin from harsh detergents. You'll need two soft, clean flannels, a warmed towel, some Fairtrade cotton wool, a little organic olive oil, and a warm room.

1 Undress your baby to the waist. Wipe her face and around her neck creases carefully with a damp, warm flannel. Dry with a warmed towel. Wipe each eye very gently from the centre outwards with separate pieces of moistened cotton wool. Repeat on her nostrils, if necessary.

2 If your baby's hair needs freshening up, dampen the flannel and wipe from the front of her head to the nape of her neck. Repeat until clean. Pat dry with a warm towel.

3 Wipe your baby's hands and under her arms with the flannel. Carefully pat dry. If your baby has areas of dry skin, rub on some organic olive oil. Clothe her upper body.

4 Undress your baby from the waist down. Moisten another flannel and wipe her bottom from front to back. Pat dry with the towel, then rub a little olive oil on any areas of nappy rash. Put her in a clean nappy and dress her.

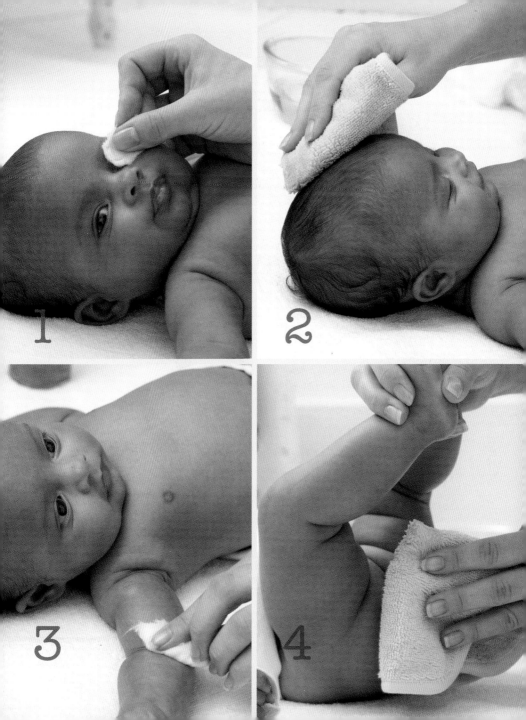

Eco baby wipe solutions

Baby wipes are one of the most wasteful products on the planet – after all, they are designed to be thrown away. Revised postnatal care guidelines in 2006 advise us not to use them for at least the first month of life. Here are greener options.

Conventional baby wipes made of bonded plastic, cellulose, and polyester don't biodegrade: each one can take several hundred years to break down, and the average baby uses up to 5,000 in her lifetime. Most conventional brands also tend to be chlorine-bleached: industrial bleaching has seriously damaged the environment and caused the release of POPs (persistant organic pollutants) that remain indefinitely in our soil, water, food, and bodies, and are linked with learning and behavioural problems.

When parents were interviewed for a 2007 report on chemicals in baby products, almost 90 per cent said that they read the ingredients labels on food, but only one-third regularly inspected skincare products. Nearly half severely underestimated the number of synthetic chemicals in even "gentle" baby wipes – there may be more than 15. These include the skin-irritating SLS (sodium lauryl sulphate), synthetic fragrances, propylene glycol (which enhances the penetration of other chemicals into the skin), oestrogen-mimicking parabens, and pesticide-heavy antibacterial agents.

 **light green** Favour eco brands that are unbleached, completely biodegradable and flushable, made with purified water and cleansing agents derived from sugar and vegetable oils, and with organic skin-soothing botanicals, such as aloe vera. Use them mainly for trips out rather than home use. Buying refill packs means 90 per cent less packaging.

mid green Make your own wipes from one of the myriad online recipes, using a roll of unbleached, recycled kitchen roll, cider vinegar, calendula oil, and aloe vera. Store in an old plastic wipe box. Alternatively, buy a diluted sea-water spray, spritz on to an organic cotton cloth, and use to wipe bottom or hands. Or make your own wipe-spray (see pp106–107) and store in the fridge in a reusable glass bottle.

deep green Gently clean your baby's bottom with toilet paper marked with the FSC (Forest Stewardship Council) logo, dispose of in the toilet, then wipe with a washable organic flannelette cloth moistened with plain water (throw it in the nappy bucket). For sticky hands and faces, moisten another clean, organic cloth (if you're going out, it's easily transported in a waterproof bag).

Every single week, a baby will get
through, on average, 42
disposable nappies

In the UK alone, around
9 million disposables are
dumped in landfills
each day

Greener nappies

Change your baby into reusable nappies, and you can change the world at the same time by greatly reducing landfill waste and carbon emissions.

Most of the waste a baby generates derives from disposable nappies, which make up a significant portion of a family's rubbish. This enormous amount of waste can take 200–500 years to decompose – imagine all the untreated sewage and harmful methane produced by the billions of nappies in landfill sites (nappies are the third largest global contributor to landfill sites).

    The energy and resources consumed in the manufacture of disposable nappies are also considerable, since they are made largely from polypropylene plastic and bleached, pulped wood. The chemical load of conventional disposable nappies often includes: superabsorbent granules of sodium polyacrylate (banned from tampons for health reasons), bactericides, pesticides, and deodorant chemicals that have been associated with skin irritation and allergic reactions.

    Despite claims to the contrary (mainly from disposable nappy companies), reusable nappies are kinder by far to the environment, and to your baby's skin. Real nappies can reduce your climate-change impact by a quarter. And you're likely to need nappies for fewer months, too: babies who wear washables tend to potty-train earlier (they learn what it's like to feel wet from an early age).

CHOOSING A NAPPY

So which washables will you choose? Organic cotton, bamboo, and hemp are sound eco options. As well as being the world's most green crops (see p37), bamboo and hemp are naturally antibacterial and hypoallergenic. Bamboo absorbs 60 per cent more moisture than cotton and does it more quickly than cotton (the nappies dry twice as fast, too), while hemp improves in absorbency and softness with washing. Silk nappy liners wick away moisture from skin better than other fabrics; and soft woollen outer-wraps offer natural water-resistance, breathability, and antibacterial properties, and often can be aired rather than washed.

Washable nappies are the cheapest green nappy option, saving the average family at least £500 even after laundry costs – with an even greater saving if you use them on subsequent babies. Most modern washable nappies are shaped like disposables, with easy fasteners and no need for expertise in origami, and there are sizes to suit every infant, from premature babies to chubby toddlers. Look out for "nappachino" events in local cafés, where you can discuss washable options and take a look at different types while having a coffee and meeting like-minded parents. You might even find that your local authority offers interest-free loans for buying a set of cloth nappies.

Many green families use nappy-washing services that deliver a set of freshly laundered cotton nappies to the door each week and take away the soiled ones. This type of service generally costs more than washing your own (about the same price you would spend on disposables per week). It may also use less energy than home washing and saves you doing the laundry.

Realistically, there may be times you find it is not practical to use a washable nappy. Completely biodegradable disposables are the latest development in green nappies. They look and work like regular disposables, but are made up of layers of unbleached cellulose filled with minimal amounts of absorbent gel and renewable absorbents, such as starch. Some biodegradable disposables are guaranteed free from harmful dioxins and chemicals such as formaldehyde, and suit babies with eczema. These nappies are highly biodegradable, but only in an earthworm composter; they don't decompose as easily if you discard them into waste that ends up in a landfill.

It takes 3.5 times more energy to manufacture disposable rather than reusable nappies

CLEANSING LOTION

This all-natural baby cleansing lotion can take the place of baby wipes: spritz it on to Fairtrade unbleached cotton wool or washable cloths, and use it to clean your baby's bottom at nappy changes.

1 Pour freshly boiled water into a tea-pot containing two organic camomile tea-bags – if you prefer, you can use a loose-leaf camomile infusion instead. Leave the tea to steep (and cool) for 15 minutes.

2 Transfer 30ml lukewarm tea to a jug, and add 1tbsp hemp oil. If your baby is over one year old, add 1 tsp pasteurized runny honey, and whisk well.

3 Pour the mixture into a reusable glass bottle with a spray-pump top. Screw on the top, and shake well to combine all the ingredients. You can then use it immediately, or let the lotion cool fully and store it in the refrigerator.

4 At nappy-change time, spray a little of the lotion (first shaking the bottle if it has been stored) on to a piece of cotton wool or a cloth wipe, then use to clean your baby's bottom. Repeat as necessary. Make up a new batch of lotion every few days and keep refrigerated.

The green, clean baby: Greener nappies

MAKING THE CHANGE

The washable nappy system consists of three main components, which you can buy or borrow: the main nappy, the liner, and the waterproof outer-wrap.

What you need

- **Main nappy** – try several shapes and sizes to see which best suits your baby (your local "real nappy" group can help; see p186). You'll need about 24 nappies.

- **Liner** – if you are feeling conscientious, use washable liners. You may want to use a cotton or silk booster-liner for extra security at night-time, or while your baby is tiny. Four to six will be plenty. Flushable, fully biodegradable paper liners are useful for disposing of solid waste.

- **Outer-wrap** – this keeps everything together and protects clothing from leaks. You'll need about four.

- **Extras** – if the nappies don't have velcro or poppers, nappy nipper fasteners are useful. You'll also need a nappy bucket with a lid, and a tote bag to carry everything in.

nappy   **liner**   **outer-wrap**

CHANGING A WASHABLE NAPPY

The actual method of changing a reusable nappy is almost identical to that of a disposable, except that there are a few more components to deal with.

1 Lay your baby on the changing mat. Remove the dirty nappy. Put the booster-liner (if using) and the nappy into the nappy bucket, and then flush the paper liner away. Put the nappy wrap to one side. Add 2 tsp bicarbonate of soda to the bucket and fill with water, then put on the lid.

2 Lifting your baby's feet in one hand, wipe her bottom using Fairtrade unbleached organic cotton wool or an unbleached cotton washable wipe or muslin square dampened with water only. Discard the cotton wool or place the dirty wipe into the nappy bucket. Pat your baby's bottom dry with a muslin square. If needed, smear on a thin layer of an organic barrier cream to prevent nappy rash.

3 Place a clean booster-liner (if using) inside a clean nappy and fold. Lay the flushable liner on top. Slide under your baby by lifting her feet, then secure the nappy using the nappy fastenings or a "nappy nipper".

4 Adjust the fastenings of the outer-wrap to ensure a snug fit over the nappy.

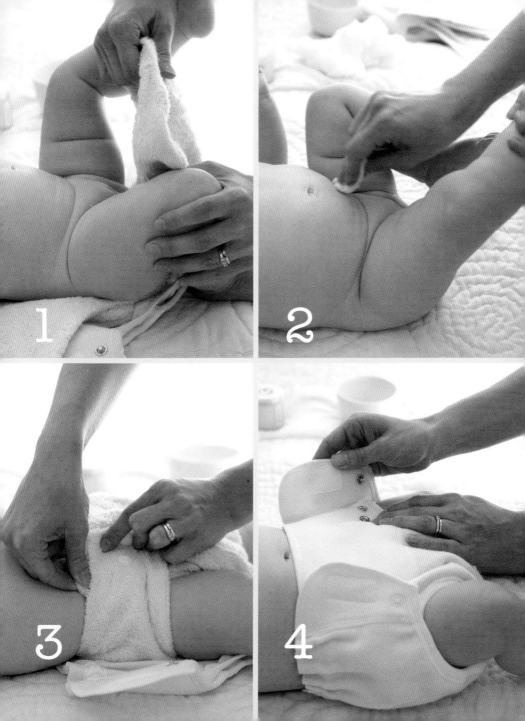

Eco nappy solutions

Many parents use a mix of green nappy systems, using compostable disposables at night or when out and about, and washables at home.

The secret to keeping reusable nappies green is not to wash them at too high a temperature. Try washing mostly at 40°C (104°F), with a little eco-washing powder or eco-balls. Avoid regular powders; many contain optical brighteners, and fabric conditioner, too: both stick to fabric, making it less absorbent and more likely to bring about a rash. Gentle handwashing is the best way to deal with woollen outer-wraps (though felted wool can be machine-washed on a cold-water wool setting). You don't have to wash these too often, since the lanolin in wool is naturally antibacterial. Avoid tumble-drying washable nappies and their outer-wraps; it can shrink and shred the fabric, causing the waterproof wraps to disintegrate. Dry outdoors whenever possible – sunlight is a powerful bleaching agent.

The greenest nappy option might make you gasp: not to use nappies at all, a technique used in many parts of the world. Known as elimination communication or timing, this involves tuning in with your baby's routine, and noticing her gestures and facial and verbal expressions when she is about to pee or poo (so you can catch it in a potty!). Advocates value the intimacy and mutual responsiveness this method establishes.

light green Use disposables that really are disposable: compostable eco-nappies (don't forget to compost the packaging, too). Look into setting up a home composting system using earthworms (vermicomposting). Or, there may be a scheme that picks up from your door for central earthworm composting. Avoid encasing these nappies in nappy bags (biodegradable or not).

mid green Use washable nappies and have them washed by a nappy laundry service. Alternatively, wash them yourself with an eco-washing powder in an "A"-rated washing-machine. If the nappies are second-hand, give yourself a pat on the back, and keep hanging them out to dry (rather than tumble-drying) so that they last long enough to pass on to another baby.

deep green Join the nappy-free movement by avoiding nappies as often as you can, and embracing elimination timing before your baby is six months old. The benefits are obvious – no nappies, no extra washing, no detergents, no nappy-rash creams, and perhaps best of all, no cost! Many one-year-olds whose parents use this method are fully potty-trained in their second year.

Green nursery: a safer space to sleep and grow

Green sleep options

Don't be disheartened if after spending time and money decorating a baby's room the eco way, you find her sharing your room for the first few months. This can be the greenest option of all, since it uses fewest resources.

Sound sleeping boosts immunity naturally in babies and exhausted parents

Does your baby even need a separate nursery? Studies suggest that babies who sleep in a cot in the same room as their parents for the first six months of life have a reduced risk of SIDS (sudden infant death syndrome). Some parents like to take this further and share their *bed* with the baby, and research finds that babies who sleep this way wake less in the night and settle back to sleep more quickly. Many breastfeeding mothers swear that this method of sleeping makes night feeds a doddle; studies back this up – although breastfed babies who sleep with their mothers feed more often, they disturb their mothers less. However, a 2004 study found that this method of sleeping, known as co-sleeping, slightly increased the risk of SIDS.

Health visitors therefore insist on a few rules: no cigarettes, alcohol, or drugs that make you drowsy, and think again if you have a sleep disorder, such as sleep apnoea, or if your baby was premature or small at birth. It's advised that you make a safe space for the baby at the top of the mattress, with no pillows and her own bedding; check that there are no gaps between the head of the bed and the wall or headboard. Dress your baby lightly, since beds with lots of people in get hot (to check her temperature, touch her tummy). You might be less cramped if you invest in a cot that abuts the parental bed (see p121), so your baby has her own safe space and bedding, and you can relax rather than trying not to move all night. This arrangement is safer if you're not around, too, as you won't always want to go to bed at the same time as your baby.

Most older babies do move into their own room, and many parents report that they sleep better without the distraction of grown-ups, who may themselves welcome the freedom to read, chat, or even enjoy uninhibited sex. Don't rush out to buy a baby monitor once your baby sleeps alone (unless you live in a mansion or your baby has a chronic breathing problem). You may disturb your baby's sleep if you rush in to check on every cough.

If your baby's erratic sleep pattern is getting you down, talk to your health visitor. You might also like to visit a cranial osteopath or homeopath, or investigate baby sleep clinics that specialize in natural methods of sleep-training.

Green nursery: Green sleep options

NATURAL SOOTHING

Try these naturally soothing strategies instead of relying on sleep-inducing electronic gadgets, such as self-rocking cradles or teddies with a heart-beat.

Baby sleeping strategies

- **Darkness** – being exposed to complete darkness at night and to outdoor light in the day seems to correlate with better sleep (and growth in premature babies). Under-twos who sleep with a light on may be more likely to be shortsighted.
- **Constant noise** – many babies sleep better with regular household noise or music rather than complete silence.
- **Swaddling** – this makes tiny babies feel secure.

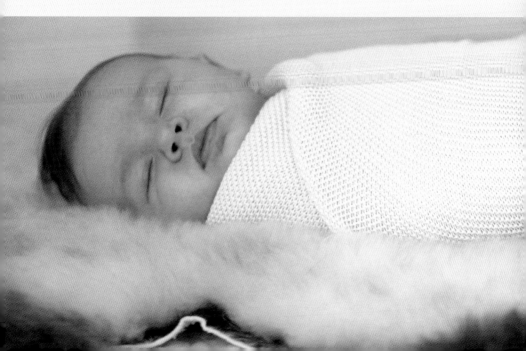

- **Ambient temperature** – aim for a room heated to 18°C (64°F) with bedding of one sheet and two layers of blanket.
- **Daytime naps** – babies who take routine naps during the day seem to sleep better at night than those who don't.
- **A set bedtime** – whether your baby seems sleepy or not: some infants become more lively the more tired they are.
- **Bedtime routine** – a consistent ritual (such as milk, bath, story, cuddle, singing) teaches a baby to anticipate sleep.
- **Put your baby to bed still awake** – he'll learn to drift off without you and so can do so again if he wakes in the night.

To swaddle your baby, lie him on a wrap, then fold one side across his body, tucking the excess under his arm; repeat on the other side.

COTS AND CRIBS

During the first three years, a baby spends more time asleep than awake, so where he sleeps is an especially important consideration in your green home.

Your baby's first sleeping place might be a Moses basket next to your bed rather than a full-sized cot in his own room. These baskets are made of biodegradable, renewable materials, such as palm and wicker. If a basket your baby will grow out of within weeks seems an unnecessary expense (and a waste of resources), borrow one, or choose a sturdy wicker version to use later as a toy basket or doll's bed. Favour baskets made from renewable local materials, with handles for carrying. Although regular carrycots are another cosy option, they tend to be made of plastic, especially if part of a pram or playpen, and may require a separate mattress for night-time. Wooden cribs tend to last longer than Moses baskets, but they aren't as readily portable. You might like to try a cheap, fully recyclable eco-crib made of cardboard which is easy to assemble and reassemble for nights away from home, though do ask how it achieves its fire retardance, and consider its durability.

Hammocks have been an infant's ideal first bed for centuries in many cultures. As the baby moves, he gently rocks himself, and the fabric cocoons him in womb-like security, while supporting his head in a position that may help to prevent reflux.

Hammocks can be soothing for colicky babies and also prevent infants from rolling on to their fronts (supine is the recommended sleeping position to reduce risk of SIDS). Specially designed baby hammocks are used in special-care baby units in hospitals around the world because of these unique features.

When choosing a cot, look for multi-functions that extend its life-span, such as a removable side that allows the cot to abut the parental bed or a design that turns into a toddler bed or sofa. Solid wood from managed, renewable sources is best, and ask suppliers about non-toxic varnishes and finishes rather than man-made sealants: your baby will soon start chewing the bars.

In two US studies, only organic cotton crib mattresses had no toxic emissions

Mattresses are an especially important eco consideration, whether for a Moses basket or a cot, since most readily available mattresses are made from polyurethane foam and PVC. Both harm the environment in their manufacture and disposal, and may emit noxious gases such as toluene or styrene, or fire retardants shown to interfere with infant brain development. Natural mattresses are harder to source and more expensive, but much longer lasting and better for the environment. Look for those made from natural latex, coir (from coconut shells), and pure new wool, with an organic cotton cover. Natural fibres wick away moisture from the body, helping to maintain a more even temperature all night long. Natural and organic mattresses (choose Soil Association certified) are also made from materials that meet fire-safety compliance standards without being treated with fire-retardant chemicals; these build up in the body and have been linked with childhood learning and behavioural problems.

Cots and mattresses are costly to purse and planet, so conserve both by sourcing them second-hand. Although studies have linked toxic bacteria in used mattresses with SIDS, the Foundation for the Study of Infant Deaths states that any mattress is OK as long as it's firm, not sagging, and doesn't show wear and tear. First, consider the factors below.

Second-hand cot safety checklist

- Reject cots with cracks, broken slats, cut-out decoration, or protruding bolts or posts. Look for safety number DOEN710.
- Check the space between the bars is less than 60mm ($2\frac{3}{8}$ in).
- Avoid if the base isn't firm or the sides don't lock upright.
- Check for peeling paint and avoid pre-1980s painted cots.
- Make sure the mattress fits snugly on all four sides.
- Does the mattress have a top layer you can detach to wash at 60°C (140°F) or higher? If not, vaccuum well to kill dust mites.

Moses baskets are ideal for very young babies as they are highly portable and make your baby feel snug and secure.

Green nursery: Green sleep options

Asthma and allergic conditions

are associated primarily

with exposure to

indoor contaminants

Regular cot and crib

mattresses may be treated with

fire retardants

that can also affect brain function

GREEN BEDDING

Buying baby bed-linen is an eco shopper's paradise; there's a virtual superstore of green options, from super-soft organic cotton to silk.

Organic cotton sheets and cellular blankets are recommended for babies under one year. Look for Fairtrade options, extra-soft pima cotton, or Demeter-certified organic wool blankets. Don't be put off by the ivory colour; it shows that the fabric hasn't been treated with harsh chlorine bleach. You might like an organic cotton mattress pad if using a second-hand or conventional mattress. Bamboo is an even more eco-friendly option for sheets, since it is softer, more hypoallergenic, and stays drier than cotton.

Many parents prefer baby sleeping-bags to sheets and blankets. Put your baby to bed in his sleepsuit and a bag that is suitable for the season (they vary in thickness). Bags are great for wriggly babies – they can enjoy having a good kick, but can't kick off the covers and so stay snug all night (which means less night waking for all of you). Look for bags made from organic cotton or soft merino wool, which adjusts naturally to the temperature of the baby and the room.

In your baby's second year (but not before), he might like to have an organic cotton pillow and a duvet. Organic wool and silk are the best duvet options for temperature control, and are also naturally hypoallergenic.

Green nursery: Green sleep options

Eco bedding solutions

Baby sleeping-bags, blankets, swaddling robes – with so many bedding options on offer, how do you select the greenest choice?

The push to produce cheap textiles in the last decade has led to some unethical trade practices, including sweat-shop conditions and child labour. How can you avoid supporting this? Choosing certified organic goods is a good start, but not the whole story, since this only guarantees the raw ingredients. To be sure that the weaving and manufacturing of fabric is as ethical as its growing, look for the SKAL logo, a sign of ethical textile processing, or the Öko Tex mark, which indicates that processing practices have minimal environmental impact and that products are of high quality (its standards for baby clothes are more stringent than for other textiles). You might also look for the FWF (Fair Wear Foundation) logo, which shows that textiles have been produced in fair-labour conditions; those marked Fairtrade only certify that producers were given a fair wage for the raw material, and don't cover processing and manufacturing stages.

At home, try to buy from small local producers. The best might buy wool from farmers who struggle to make a profit from traditional farming, then employ women with skills that are fast being lost to knit clothes and blankets using traditional patterns and techniques, preserving our heritage for future generations.

light green

Buy brand-new, unbleached, certified organic cotton sheets and you can reassure yourself that few artificial fertilizers and pesticides were used by those who farm the crops. This protects the soil and water sources, as well as the health of the farmer and his family. And you can guarantee that your baby won't spend hours lying on fabric that contains pesticide residues.

mid green

Borrow, or buy second-hand if you can't borrow, an organic cotton baby sleeping-bag or two (a light-weight version for summer and a warmer one for winter), then forget about top sheets or blankets. Merino wool bags require less washing (simply air them outdoors), but if your baby is allergy-prone, choose one that can be washed at 60°C (140°F) to kill dust mites.

deep green

Get your granny to knit a baby blanket from wool from British farms, or ask friends to meet up for a knitting evening to knit a square each to sew into a baby blanket, or to patch-work off-cuts of cotton into a quilt (not suitable for young babies). Look for vintage linen sheets at antique textile fairs woven from plants raised before the days of pesticides; they're likely to be of good quality.

Decorating the nursery

The urge to nest has many of us stripping walls, sanding floors, and redecorating before a baby arrives. But you need to protect your baby's health and the environment.

When you're pregnant or have a small baby, don't stay at home while rooms are being sanded or stripped of old paint; the dust may contain hazardous toxins, such as lead, which was added to paint until the 1970s. It's best to have someone else do the dirty work and clean up afterwards, and to get major work done well in advance of the baby's arrival. Do wait for a few weeks and air a newly decorated room very well before allowing a baby to sleep in it. A new paint smell indicates the presence of the climate-changing chemicals known as VOCs (volatile organic compounds). These chemical solvents include toluene, exposure to which increases the risk of neurological and developmental problems. VOCs also trigger headaches and have been associated with post-natal depression. They are off-gassed by paint for years. Recent EU regulations have resulted in fewer VOCs in paint, but also in the addition of dangerous replacement chemicals, such as ammonia, acetone, and biocides, and more energy-intensive production processes. How do you choose a better paint? Avoid those made by multinational chemical companies (most paint in

DIY stores). Buy instead from small manufacturers that specialize in natural paint, declare their environmental standards, and list the ingredients on the tin. Most eco-paints are low in VOCs or have none at all, and have fewer man-made chemicals than regular paints. Those that win German eco prizes are good; when ordering, ask about nursery-grade options.

Carpets and PVC-backed flooring are the second-most-potent source of toxins at home after paint. If you can, remove them completely from a baby's room. If you don't like bare

PVC flooring in a child's room is the strongest single cause of respiratory ailments

boards, fit linoleum (which is made from linseed oil and is completely biodegradable), or flooring woven from bamboo or grasses (choose natural backing and have it fitted the old-fashioned way with nails not glue). If you can't do without carpet, choose 100 per cent untreated wool. It's biodegradable, naturally fire-resistant, remains soft for years, and even purifies the room (wool absorbs airborne contaminants such as formaldehyde, and binds them in for up to 30 years). Wool is allergenic; research suggests it resists dust mites more effectively than nylon carpet.

NURSERY FURNISHINGS

Once you've redecorated your baby's room, you'll want to fit it out with non-toxic, environmentally-friendly furnishings that will last.

Think about the big furniture first – a cupboard or wardrobe for storing baby clothing and toys, nappies and changing materials; perhaps a toddler-sized table and chairs; a rocking chair for feeds; and a bookcase. Question whether you need a changing station; you're unlikely to use it after the first year, and it's safer to change your child on the floor on a plastic-free changing mat. Green shoppers opt for solid wood furniture from forests managed sustainably. The FSC certification stamp guarantees that the wood in your furniture can be traced back to a forest managed in an environmentally responsible and socially beneficial way. Also consider wooden items made from newer green materials, such as bamboo or coconut. It's greener still to buy furniture made from reclaimed timber, and greenest of all to fill your home with pre-loved furniture – buying second-hand

Every day in the UK, at least
3,000 tonnes
of reusable wood are
burned or sent to landfill

saves trees and energy, and makes your home look unique in an era of cheap, fashion-led furnishing. Buying locally sourced and made pieces saves wood miles, too. Most furniture has a high carbon footprint because it's so bulky to transport.

Chemical-free is the only way to go with babies, so avoid composite-wood furniture, which is manufactured by gluing together thin slices of wood with adhesives that may contain (and off-gas) formaldehyde and other chemical nasties. Avoid also anything that might have been varnished with man-made chemical finishes. To be extra sure furniture won't off-gas VOCs, look for items made the old-fashioned way, using mortise and tenon joints – no glues or even screws or nails. Bespoke eco-furniture designed and made in the UK may be high in price, but if you buy just one piece you adore, you're more likely to cherish and preserve it for many years, which you might not do with a flimsy flat-pack item – and this saves money (in the long-term) as well as the planet. If you're ditching old flat-pack furniture, look for an organization that will repair and redistribute it, rather than dumping it at the tip.

Instead of rushing out to buy all-new eco curtains, cushions, and rugs, see what you can revamp and customize from elsewhere. Then search out furnishing fabrics in organic cotton, robust hemp, or jute. Reserve a good part of your budget for thick-lined curtains that keep out the light and keep in warmth. Draw them at dusk to save around £15 a year on heating bills.

Green nursery: Decorating the nursery

Hemp is a particularly effective insulating material, said to have the best heat-ratio capacity of any natural fibre. It also resists fading from light. When buying fabric to make your own curtains, ask about the chemicals used to print and dye it, and decline finishes such as permanent pressing and stain-guards, which may coat the fabric in chemicals thought to damage immunity and reproductive hormones. PVC blackout backing is another no-no. As well as damaging the environment with chlorine and dioxins, studies link PVC and its plasticizing chemicals with childhood respiratory problems and asthma.

The all-natural soft furnishing your baby will love most is a lambskin for luxurious lounging. As ever, choose local and unbleached if you can; some skins are tanned with mimosa rather than harsh chemicals, others might be guaranteed free from organophosphates (nerve agents used in sheep-dip) or heavy metals used in conventional tanning. Buying direct from a farm guarantees income for struggling sheep farmers, and you might pick up an interesting skin from a heritage breed. They resist stains and are self-cleansing, but can be machine washed in cool water. Lying on a lambskin (which is naturally warm in winter and cool in summer) seems to soothe babies and to encourage better sleep, contentment, and weight gain.

Use wooden furniture from sustainable sources and fabrics made from natural materials for your child's nursery.

Green nursery: Decorating the nursery

Play green: natural ways to learn and have fun

The mini-consumer

It's easy to get sucked into a world of primary-coloured plastic and "baby-genius" toys after giving birth. Here's how and why to resist the pressure.

Even before a baby is born, the pressure's on for us to brand her room, wardrobe, and toy-box with the licensed characters of film and TV. This helps to create a throwaway mentality and acquisitive brand awareness from birth, since each new set of merchandise makes the last one redundant. Aggressive marketing targets parents and children, driving the consumer mill. Why is this bad for the planet as well as our children's health? Manufacturing, transportation, and disposal (most toys are made from petrochemicals in China and can't be recycled) all eat up ancient forest and fossil fuels and emit climate-change gases. Worries centre around PVC, one of the forms of plastic most often used in toy-making; when made or incinerated, PVC emits dioxins – carcinogens that build up in soil, water, food, and our bodies. Health concerns also surround the plasticizing chemicals that make PVC soft, especially phthalates, which may easily leach out – Danish studies on teething rings found "significant migration" of phthalates. Initial studies link them with damage to the reproductive system, kidneys, and liver, and also to asthma. The US EPA (Environment Protection Agency) regards one phthalate, called DEHP, as a "probable human carcinogen". So concerned is the EU that in January 2007 it banned three phthalates (DEHP, DBP, BBP) from toys and childcare products in concentrations of more than 0.1 per cent. Three more (DINP, DIDP, DNOP) were banned from any toys that under-threes put in their mouths. Other potentially dangerous additives in plastic toys include organotins (which can disrupt testosterone), nonylphenol (can damage immunity), and the toxic heavy metals cadmium and lead. Some toys for the very young have tested positive for harmful fire retardants. But don't bin Barbie; she might leach toxins into landfills or into the air if incinerated. Don't recycle her either. Not all toys are marked with a plastic number (only those numbered "2", "4", or "5" can be recycled) and those without spoil all the plastic in a batch.

Research shows that children as young as 18 months old can recognize brands

You are probably not responsible for the pile of plastic toys suffocating your mini-consumer. Most likely, they rain in from adoring friends and family. Why not suggest that the best gift of all is for these people to spend time with your child – to take her to the park, a toddler swim session, or puppet show. When stuff is so omnipresent, giving time is a thoughtful way to show love.

Play green: The mini-consumer

In the UK, we discard more than
44 million
functioning **toys**
each year,
many made from **PVC**
which releases
noxious gases
into **landfills**

Manufacture of toys

Many green parents like to consider how and where a toy was made as well as what materials it's made from.

Most toys made outside Europe are produced in China (which manufactures some 80 per cent of the world's toys) on behalf of multinational companies. Though working conditions are improving, they are not ideal on many sites where working time and pay-regulation directives may not be enforced. The seasonal nature of our buying habits also has an impact, leading to periods of excessive working hours followed by unemployment. There is concern that a drop in toy prices in the past ten years (by 33 per cent in the US), despite the rising prices of raw materials, is largely made possible by cheap labour. The trend towards cost-cutting has also been linked to the safety recall in 2007 of millions of toys made in China that had powerful detachable magnets and were contaminated with lead paint.

What can you do? Write to your favourite toy manufacturer telling them that you care about the workers who make your child's toys, asking about measures they are taking to ameliorate conditions. If you don't get a satisfactory answer, stop buying their toys, and talk to your friends about your decision. Why not begin a blog? People underestimate consumer power, but if you let your views be known, you may be surprised at the results.

Greener toys

The good news is that toys don't have to be made of plastic, and there is a wide selection of green options available.

Naturally germ-resistant, durable, and fully degradable, wooden toys are the most obvious choice for an ethical consumer. Choose solid (not particle) wood from sustainable sources (note the FSC logo) and check that varnishes and paints are non-toxic, water-based, and free of VOCs (volatile organic compounds). Linseed, walnut oil, and beeswax are non-toxic alternative coatings.

Natural materials make toys appealing and sustainable.

Handmade toys have a prized place among your baby's toys.

Be vigilant about teethers and rattles: untreated natural wood may be best. Sustainable rubberwood is a good choice; it comes from trees felled at the end of their latex production life. If the wood is indigenous and the toy locally made, perhaps by people without much paid work, give yourself a big green tick. Recycled, biodegradable cardboard toys are fun, too, even though they are designed to be thrown away.

Hemp or organic cotton cuddly toys are popular with babies. Since they get sucked and hugged to sweaty bodies, be sure the dyes are environment- and baby-friendly (the Öko-Tex logo guarantees this). Teddies stuffed and finished with organic wool suit children prone to allergies, as wool deters dust mites.

Non-toxic paints are vital for toys that may be chewed.

Long-lasting toys can be passed on as family heirlooms.

MAKING YOUR OWN TOYS

It may be hard to resist pressures to buy toys, but with a little effort you can show your child what fun it can be to improvise toys from household items.

Home-made toys tend to foster open-ended creative play – the unstructured play crucial to infant learning. Researchers find that toys which direct play, such as electronic gadgets that require children to press buttons or give right and wrong answers, may discourage creativity, undermine basic motor skills, and shorten attention span. They also set up a barrier to social interaction. To stimulate these childhood essentials, spend time together improvising toys from household objects. Make a doll from a wooden spoon by drawing on a face with non-toxic pens and tying a fabric dress around its "neck". As your baby grows, graduate to home-made peg- and rag-dolls. Throw together a dressing-up box of cast-offs and cut-downs. Make your own play-dough (search online for a recipe for an edible version): polymer clays contain PVC, and phthalates have been found on children's hands even after washing. The most ethical toys are your child's own fingers and toes: explore them with songs or a book of counting rhymes.

Home-made toys are fun to make and foster your child's resourcefulness and creativity, without costing much.

MAKING A TREASURE BASKET

Natural and household objects are an easy way to encourage your baby's sensory exploration when she can sit steadily. Fill a basket with objects of varying texture, colour, size, and shape.

1 First, look for hard objects. They must be large enough to handle and suck without risk of swallowing. Try smooth pebbles, shells, and twigs; shiny surfaces, such as metal cups; objects for threading (like wooden curtain rings), or that stack inside each other (like Russian dolls).

2 Now find soft objects: long, clean feathers, a leather key fob, sheep's wool, leaves; fabrics such as velvet, silk, linen, and felt (make them into bags to put objects into and take out); small wicker baskets for sorting like with like.

3 Add some natural scents: a lavender bag or pine cones, or put cinnamon sticks or vanilla pods in a spice-shaker. Create noise with coconut shells, jingling metal bangles, a bunch of keys, or hand bells.

4 Stay with your baby while she explores her treasures, ask what happens if she shakes or smells them, and add new items regularly to keep her interest alive.

Play green: Greener toys

SECOND-HAND TOYS

"Share and repair" is the mantra for green parents – and one worth passing on to your children. When you fancy a new toy for your child, just think second-hand.

Because we buy so many toys – each Christmas, British children unwrap £2 billion worth – there is a huge number of unwanted quality toys in circulation. Instead of buying brand new, start your search at the local car-boot fair, National Childbirth Trust sales, or charity shops, and browse newspaper small ads and Freecycle emails. Try second-hand baby shops, which vet toys for safety. If you don't find what you want, go global with online auction sites.

Supporting second-hand exchange is a two-way transaction. Rather than discarding toys your child has grown out of, find them a new home. Sort through the toy-box before birthdays or Christmas, and bag up items your child has out-grown before the next deluge arrives. Sort them into three piles: one to put away as heirlooms or keepsakes, or pass on to siblings and cousins; one to sell online or at a car-boot sale; and one to donate to a charity shop, hospital, doctor's surgery, or playgroup. Encourage toddlers to help; it makes the task longer and potentially tearful, but starts them thinking about the worth of objects and what happens to stuff they no longer need. Some manufacturers of large toys, such as plastic kitchens or garden equipment, take back items for recycling. Try out your local toy library, too, where you can borrow new toys every week for free and socialize with other parents.

Play green: Greener toys

Long-lasting second-hand buys include collections that can be added to, for constant rekindling of the urge to play, and durable solid wood and metal objects. The CE and Lion marks show toys meet current safety standards. What's best avoided? Take the sniff test; if a toy smells like new plastic, it's full of phthalates. Don't buy pre-1980s painted items (may contain lead), toys with fluid or electronic components, and damaged goods.

Even **ethical toys** stop being ethical if they end up discarded in a **landfill site**

Covetable second-hand toys

- **Lego** – indestructible and it's free of phthalates; no PVC policy.
- **Playmobil** – for older toddlers; no PVC policy.
- **Käthe Kruse dolls** – handcrafted dolls made of wood and cloth that can be repaired in the German factory.
- **Brio train set** – choose wood, though all Brio is PVC-free.
- **IKEA toys** – free from PVC, and dodgy woods and dyes.
- **Wooden dolls' house, fort, or puppet theatre** – finding the accessories and dolls separately adds to the adventure.
- **Metal construction toys** – durable and can be added to.

CLEANING TOYS

Involve your toddler in cleaning and repairing her own toys and she will learn very early that taking care and mending lengthen the lifespan of her favourite things.

Cleaning toys can be a fun activity to do together. Lay newspaper on the floor or work outdoors, then fill one bowl with warm soapy water (use an eco washing-up liquid) and another with plain warm water. You'll also need two wooden scrubbing brushes, dishcloths, and dry towels. Dump the toys in the soapy water and scrub well, then rinse in the clean water, and dry with a towel. Peg up dolls' clothes or soft toys to dry outdoors. It's best to avoid bleach or antibacterial soap, wipes, and sprays. Antibacterial cleaners are no more effective than soap and water, and may contain the antimicrobial pesticide triclosan (highly toxic if it enters the marine environment). They may also contain denatured ethanol, an irritant to eyes and mucous membranes. The residue from sprays lingers on surfaces and toys, ready to transfer to tiny fingers and mouths.

To rid soft toys and woollen items of dust mites and wool moths, place them in a plastic bag and freeze for a few days, then machine-wash with eco washing powder at 60°C (140°F), or 30°C (86°F) for wool, and hang up to dry outside.

Getting wet is all part of the fun when your toddler helps to keep his toys clean.

Play green: Greener toys

Eco toy solutions

There are so many environment-friendly toys available that it's easy to slip into an unethical shopping fest and buy too much. The greenest rule of toy-buying might be to buy nothing at all!

To be sure that the toy manufacturers you buy from have ethical practices, only buy toys made in the EU or from Fairtrade projects. Plastic toys from outside the EU may contain phthalates banned here, and it's tricky to tell if they do because so many aren't marked with a plastic number. The most ethical way to buy new toys is to choose soft toys and solid wooden toys handcrafted locally. They might not be organic or use recycled materials, but they cut down on toy miles, allow you to opt out of multinational trading if you find it distasteful, and, importantly, present your child with something original. Offering an alternative to mass-marketed products may help to offset the anxiety children can suffer when involved in consumer culture.

In the end, if every moment becomes a green shopping or learning opportunity, even ethical toys become just another part of the same consumer pressure. The greenest act of all is not to buy or acquire anything for a while and instead to spend time with your baby with no objects at all. Rather than guiding this free-play session, simply look at your baby and react to her prompts as she sets the agenda for what you do.

light green Buy a Fairtrade toy, such as the educational toys produced by families in Sri Lanka for Lanka Kada: this project supplies year-round employment and cuts out middlemen. Such producers tend to avoid PVC and excess packaging, as they do not want to waste resources. Buying a Fairtrade toy for your baby means that it has not been made in a sweatshop by another child.

mid green Play with Lego. As it's made of plastic, it might seem a curious eco choice, but children play with it for around ten years and it's durable enough to pass down the generations. Second-hand Lego is rare, proof of how highly parents and kids rate it. Unlike most plastic toys, it doesn't emit noxious fumes and the manufacturer has impressive waste- and energy-minimizing policies.

deep green Make a playhouse from a cardboard box. Cut holes for windows and doors, then play peekaboo, a toxin-free, eco-friendly way to entertain infants. When your baby gets bored, tear it up and compost or send it off in your kerbside collection. Make another a month or two later. Or, sew your own soft toy from cast-offs, stuffing it with scraps of fabric. There are no rules; let your imagination take flight.

Introducing books

Babies who "read" books with their parents tend to demonstrate enhanced language skills, focus, motivation, and concentration, and have a head-start in reading when they go to school.

However, a 2007 study found that primary-school children in the UK spend twice as long watching TV as reading with an adult. To cut your family's future carbon footprint, start the reading habit young and thus reduce TV use – you can introduce your baby to colourful picture books from birth. She may become so excited by the activity that within a few months she'll be batting the pages of favourite board books in her eagerness to get to the next picture. Do read books of rhymes and lullabies with your baby too. Nursery rhymes are especially good because they imprint rhythms and sound patterns in your baby's brain that mirror those of speech. Books also help your baby to learn how to listen. Reading may be as valuable for bonding as for brain development because it's something you do together; sharing a book is a special time of cosy one-to-one interaction.

Join your local **library**, one of the most enjoyable ways to **reuse** books

Unlike other forms of entertainment, like watching TV or listening to music, you can't read and do anything else at the same time. Intensify the bonding process by setting aside a few minutes for reading at the same time every day, and by making the space really cosy. Sit in a comfy chair and snuggle your baby into your lap. She'll soon begin to associate books with relaxation, which may be why reading makes such a calming addition to a bedtime routine. When reading to a baby, put on a sing-song voice, adopt funny voices for different characters, and improvise your own details (you don't have to stick to the printed text). Point out pictures with your finger. If you find any of this difficult or embarrassing, see if there's a baby book group at your local library. The library's literacy development worker can help to build your confidence. Join the library while you're there for an endless, inherently green supply of new books.

What about educational DVDs specially engineered to boost your baby's intelligence? The hard sell might make you feel guilty if you don't use them. If you prefer to cut your carbon footprint and keep the TV off, you'll be reassured by a University of Washington study that found a large and statistically significant reduction in vocabulary among infants aged 8–16 months who watched baby DVDs or videos. Other research into babies and language development found that electronic tools weren't as effective in promoting early literacy as sharing a book, and led to a "severely truncated" reading experience.

Play green: Introducing books

CHOOSING GREENER BOOKS

Your baby will suck any book she can grasp, so if you can, choose those that are less toxic. The publishing industry is beginning to tackle environmental concerns and bring us greener books.

The greenest books are "eco-printed" using non-metal inks on 100 per cent post-consumer recycled chlorine-free paper, with presses that minimize solvent use or don't require copper plates. Green printers may also use renewable energy in printing and shipping. But these kinds of books can be hard to find.

Key features of green books

• **FSC certification** – this shows that the paper has been sourced from responsibly managed forests. Favour paper with at least 50 per cent post-consumer recycled content.

• **Greener inks** – look for soy- and vegetable-based inks.

• **Water-based glues** – books with less adhesive are safer.

• **Less bleaching** – find books that are "processed chlorine-free" (PCF), which substitute oxygen-based compounds instead.

• **Avoid plastic** – it might be wise to avoid bath books altogether. They tend to be made from non-renewable petrochemicals made bendy with phthalates.

Read about the environment with your baby from the start, and he'll grow up eager to preserve it.

Every year in the UK, we deposit up to **300 million batteries** in landfill sites

Battery leakage of heavy metals, such as **mercury** and **lead**, can be **toxic** to the environment

Minimizing energy use

To cut your baby's carbon emissions and
production of toxic waste, say "no" to toys
with batteries or transformers.

Batteries are an all-round hassle, whether you hate the
noise of battery-operated toys, find buying new ones a constant
nuisance, worry about old batteries corroding, or just don't know
how to dispose of them. If we can't replace batteries, or get tired
of the expense of doing so, toys lose their appeal, which brings
even more hassle for the green parent since it's almost
impossible to recycle battery-operated toys: the toys are made
from mixed materials and there are no UK plants that reprocess
non-lead acid batteries. (Contact your local waste team to find
out how to dispose safely of batteries.) Above all, don't throw
them in the bin; batteries leak dangerous heavy metals into the
ground at landfill sites. If you're given battery-powered toys,
take them back and exchange for something more durable, or ask
for green alternatives, like clockwork or solar-powered toys.

We waste the equivalent of two power stations' worth of
electricity each year simply by leaving the TV and electronic
gadgets on standby. Save energy by always turning off electrical
items (such as chargers and the TV or music centre) at the
socket when not in use. You might also like to consider changing
to a 100 per cent green energy tariff.

Out and about: introducing your baby to a greener world

Motor vehicles form the largest
source of global atmospheric
pollution

Transport over all
accounts for about a quarter
of the UK's
CO_2 emissions

Transporting your baby

Motor vehicles use a third of the world's oil, so how you travel makes a difference to your carbon footprint; choosing greener ways to get about can enhance your community and your baby's health.

Car use by parents is increasing more rapidly than for the rest of the UK population. Research suggests this is not only because mothers' lives are increasingly complex and time-squeezed now more of us work (and fear for children's safety), but also because of the trend for out-of-town shopping, schools, and hospitals. In addition, taking public transport with babies and children can be difficult and expensive. But your travel choices affect your baby's future: it seems that children who travel by car are less likely to walk to school and more likely to develop into car-dependent adults. The associated lack of physical activity increases the risk of heart disease, stroke, obesity, and osteoporosis.

    Think about why you travel outside your neighbourhood. Can you socialize, shop, and take baby classes nearer home to cut atmospheric pollution and get to know your local community a little better? When venturing afield on public transport, travel off-peak, and take a friend to help with buggy and bags, and to entertain a wriggly baby. Email your MP and bus company about making travel with a baby easier and hybrid/ biodiesel buses to make cities cleaner.

BABY CARRIERS

Carrying infants in a sling is the ultimate in green transportation, whether they snuggle in close as tiny babies or ride high on your back as toddlers.

Slings have far less impact on the environment than any buggy or car-seat, since they tend to be made of small amounts of cloth and few plastics or metals. They are not bulky to transport and are often made locally rather than being shipped around the globe. Baby carriers pass on easily from baby to baby without having to be safety-checked. Even better, slings seem to boost bonding and well-being. A study into babies carried for about three hours a day showed that they cried less, spent more time quiet and alert, and fed more often than non-carried babies. The physical stimulation and increased interaction that come with sling use may also boost growth and development, counter baby blues and make you feel a more confident parent. They're certainly easier on public transport than bulky buggies.

    The greenest sling is one you make yourself (find a pattern online), but if you plan to borrow or buy one, try out a few (they all feel very different) at a second-hand baby items stall or organic baby shop. Look for a design that spreads weight evenly

A versatile sling that can be used to carry a baby or toddler in a range of positions will give you the longest usage. Make sure the straps are wide enough to spread weight evenly.

across your back and shoulders. The types that get used longest allow you to carry a sleeping baby lying sideways and to breastfeed discreetly, and they accommodate infants facing either inward or out, as well as toddlers on the hip and back. Organic, washable fabric is best. How do you check if the sling you like has been made according to ethical working practices? Choose one manufactured wholly in the UK or the European Union.

Which way should your baby face? It may be best to carry young babies facing inward, snuggled comfortably into your chest. The splay-hip position of many slings may help strengthen the hip joints. Inward-facing boosts interaction, too, helping your baby learn communication and language skills. Grizzly babies, however, may like the distraction of facing outward, though the rush of stimuli can be overwhelming. Older babies often enjoy a more structured frame back-pack, which suits leisure walking on account of its extra support. The longer you carry your child, the more he gets used to pedestrian transport, and is less likely to become a car-dependent adult. And you'll be a great role model for the benefits of exercise.

Babies who are **carried** seem to fuss and **cry less** in the first 3 months of life

PUSH-CHAIRS & PRAMS

Half the journeys we make are less than two miles (about three kilometres) – perfect for taking a stroll with a buggy.

However, choosing a buggy can be stressful given the many options. Standard or all-terrain stroller, travel system that morphs from car-seat to pram, forward- or backward-facing seat? Consumer studies find that most parents prefer something that's lightweight to carry and fold (especially if you often use public transport), and that fits in the car boot. Longevity is a good green measure – the best choice being one item that takes you from newborn to age four. Resource-intensive over-engineering is to be avoided: do you really need a plastic cup-holder or all-terrain rubber tyres if you only push around the local shops?

Prams can seem bulky and old-school, but have advantages. They force you to walk, since they don't pack into a car or travel well on buses, and have sufficient space for shopping. Your baby can stretch out flat (essential for newborns), nap comfortably, and, perhaps most importantly, face you. The National Literacy Trust claims that forward-facing buggies hamper a baby's developing communication skills, since he can't read your face and sounds. They also place your baby at the level of car exhausts. A buggy or pram that elevates your baby to waist height or above is healthier for your baby. The first generation of eco-prams are lined with wool and organic cotton and free from

PVC and chemical treatments. A vintage pram might be even greener: built to last, they often pass down the generations. Borrow one, then buy a buggy at six months once you know what suits you. Some options allow a baby to face you, then swivel to face forwards as he grows. Travel systems that morph from car-seat to push-chair to carrycot tend to be so complicated that parents ditch them for a lightweight buggy and a car-seat that fits a growing baby. Another problem with travel systems is that babies are so portable it's all too easy to leave them clipped in for hours as you move from car to push-chair to supermarket trolley. Free your baby well before two hours have elapsed and don't let him sleep in a car-seat for long periods: it's not great for developing

bodies to be upright (encased in plastic) for hours. Flat-head syndrome, a distortion of the cranium, is becoming more common and may result from strapping babies upright for long periods. This may also harm the spine and can lead to vomiting, low levels of blood oxygen, and breathing difficulties. The American Academy of Pediatrics advises that young babies spend minimal time in car-seats (and buggies, swings, or bouncy seats). Release your baby, cuddle him, gently stretch his limbs, put him on his front or your lap, and talk face to face – or use a sling.

A push-chair that converts from single to double by adding a seat attachment is ideal for the growing green family.

BUYING SECOND-HAND

Sales of brand-new baby goods, from slings to push-chairs and car-seats, are at an all-time high. It seems we have got out of the habit of passing on and buying second-hand. But it's a greener option.

The Ethical Consumer organization attributes the trend for buying new, in part, to the pressure from trade associations, an argument that is often presented as a matter of safety. However, it's quite safe to purchase and borrow sturdy pre-used prams and push-chairs if you follow a few rules:

Second-hand safety points

- Ensure the label shows British Standard number 7409 and the date 1996 or EU standard EN1888: 2003.
- Check that the brakes hold the pram or push-chair securely on a slope.
- Check that the wheels seem securely fixed and undamaged.
- The folding-up action should be smooth and fixed by two separate locks, with no parts or sharp edges to trap fingers.
- Look at the harness; it should have a five-point action (fitting over the shoulders, around the waist, and through the legs). Check that you can adjust the fit of the straps.
- Can you remove fabric to wash it, or replace accessories?

For car-seats, the advice from the Royal Society for the Prevention of Accidents (RoSPA) is always to buy new. However, many green parents feel happy inheriting pre-used seats if they are fairly new (and so likely to meet current safety standards) and come from a trusted source, who can guarantee that the car-seat has not been involved in an accident. Even if you can guarantee the provenance of a used seat, it's vital to examine it for damage (although you won't be able to see interior damage) and to check that it's labelled with the UN (United Nations) safety number 44.03 or .03. It's also important to have the original instructions to be able to fit the seat correctly. Decline any seat if it won't fit your car snugly or is not appropriate for your child's age and weight. Check the label: for young babies, you'll need a seat marked "Group 0" or "0+" (for infants up to 10kg/22lb or 13kg/29lb) and for older babies and toddlers, "Group I" (9–18kg/20–40lb). When buying new, check the manufacturer's website for their policy on using cadmium or lead, bromine or chlorine, phthalates, or PVC – if they don't have a policy, it might be sensible to avoid their products. You might like to make a cover in organic cotton to fit over non-organic car-seats.

A 2005 study found that the **child's seat** is the last thing most parents check after an **accident**

Out and about: Transporting your baby

JOURNEYS BY BIKE

Cycling, the second most green mode of transport after walking, is enjoying a renaissance worldwide. So don't feel you have to give up cycling now you have a baby.

Children are essential to the future of this cycling renaissance, and may be more likely to see cycling as an alternative to car journeys if they gain confidence by starting the habit young.

Babies are usually ready to start travelling on your bike once they can sit up confidently (with their head unsupported) and tolerate the weight of a helmet. For most babies this happens after their first birthday and once they reach around 9kg (20lb). You'll be able to keep your baby in a seat until he outgrows its weight limit (around 15kg/33lb or 22kg/49lb, depending on the seat), which may be well after his fourth birthday. There are seat options for the front, middle, and rear of an adult bike, as well as trailers that usually attach to the back. Even if enclosing your child between your arms on a cross-bar seat feels safer, many parents favour the rear-mounted seat,

The number of
cycle journeys
made in London has risen by
100% in 5 years

since piling weight on to the front of a bike affects the steering and balance (and a child makes the ride more unstable anyway). Trailers that carry one or two children are another option (some can even be converted into a push-chair), but, again, babies must be able to support themselves sitting upright with a helmet. This option may be best on quiet roads, cycle lanes, and country paths.

The most suitable bicycle for carrying or towing a child is a solid, reliable hybrid (a cross between a mountain and a road bike) with a good range of gears. Choose one appropriate to your region: hilly or flat, dry or wet, salty or urban grimy. For advice, consult your local independent bike dealer (IBD), other parent cyclists, and internet forums; they'll also have tips on regaining confidence if you haven't ridden for a while. If you plan to buy a second-hand bike, take a specialist along with you to vet it.

Bike manufacturing isn't as green as in the past, when bikes and their components may have been manufactured in the UK and were easily repairable. Most bikes and components are now made and assembled in Asia and the Far East, and it can be difficult and expensive to bring it up to current safety standards. And because of year-on-year technological advances, parts may not be compatible between models. For safety reasons, have your bike serviced every year; try to choose a bike workshop that recycles its tyres, metal, and packaging.

BABY CYCLING EQUIPMENT

When buying new cycling gear, make an independent bike dealer (IBD) your first port of call, and enquire about the company's ethos and the materials used.

Buy from a shop that is a member of the ACT (Association of Cycle Traders); make sure the staff are qualified, CyTech-accredited bike mechanics, and that customers are happy to recommend them. To try out different bikes, visit a bicycle hire shop and have a green family outing. Ask for advice on which type of seat is most appropriate for your child's age and size, the type of bike you ride, and your region's climate and geography.

Cycle dealers say there is no sure way of finding a safe and reliable second-hand seat. Whether you decide to buy new or second-hand, look for the EU safety mark "EN 14344: 2004", a five-point harness, and a footguard, and if you have doubts, ask your IBD to check it over and advise on affixing safely.

Helmets are something you must buy new, unless you know the history of the hat inside out. (If you have an accident, you *must* buy a new helmet.) There is a variety of sizes, paddings, and adjustments, so have your baby's helmet fitted by an expert. You might also want to invest in an anti-pollution mask for yourself, especially if you live in the city.

Start cycling in dedicated cycle lanes and on cycle trails to brush up your bike skills and give toddlers an exciting ride.

Out and about: Transporting your baby

Green places to go

Staying close to home has many merits when you have a baby, not least that it's greenest to travel only as far as you can walk or push.

You don't have to trek out to a nature reserve to have fun introducing your baby to the natural world; it's all around you. Stroll to your local park, showing your baby the sky, birds, and insects; allow him to touch bark, earth, and crunchy leaves. Take a rug and lie together looking up through the branches of a tree; he'll be fascinated by the play of light and shadow. If this is part of a weekly or daily routine, your baby will learn how the world changes through the seasons, and he'll grow to love his environment. For more adventure, try camping or green festivals (check out the compost loos and solar-powered showers).

If there's nowhere nice to walk, consider joining a campaign to transform a neglected space like a railway embankment or old industrial site into an oasis for wildlife. Or start a campaign to plant trees: each one absorbs one ton of carbon dioxide in its lifetime, improves air quality, and cuts urban heat. If roads are too traffic-choked for you to feel safe, protest with other parents by holding a "baby bloc" (read all about it online).

Taking a picnic will introduce your baby to the pleasures of enjoying food in the open air.

Car solutions

Downsizing your car use, or even giving up your car entirely, is perhaps the greenest measure you can take on your baby's behalf.

Cars begin to pollute the environment long before they hit the road; a quarter of the pollutants are thought to be released in the manufacturing process, and the effects hang around long after they've been dumped – in toxic fluids, batteries, tyres, plastics, and heavy metals – while the construction of roads endangers habitats, biodiversity, and the water table.

Do biofuels enable greener motoring? Though better for air quality, plant-based fuels are not benign. In northern climates, large-scale cultivation of plants to create bio-ethanol may require as many, or more, fossil fuels than regular fuel (for fertilizers, processing, and transportation). This also ties up agricultural land, perhaps resulting in more air-freighted food. In tropical regions, biofuels are blamed for the clearing of carbon-absorbing forests and for making staple foods, like maize, unaffordable.

To cut emissions and fuel use, first check your tyre pressures are correct and remove unnecessary roof racks or weight from the boot. Keep the windows closed and don't brake suddenly or pull away at speed. Emissions are lowest at 50mph and highest over 70mph. To reduce carbon emissions by 10 per cent, switch off the air con – and the engine if stationary for 2 minutes or more.

light green Downsize to a smaller, less-polluting, fuel-efficient car with a carbon dioxide output of less than 140g per km (see the Environmental Transport Association's buyer's guide). Why not manage with one car, or consider an electric car? Try to go car-free one day a week, or change your insurance to a restricted mileage – can you drive less than the average UK driver's 9,000 miles per year?

mid green Join a car-share scheme: each car-pool vehicle on the road replaces five privately owned cars. You could try a formal scheme or share informally with another family (perhaps instead of a second car). This cuts the cost of servicing, taxing, and insuring. Look up the emissions you puff out on each journey on a travel calculator website as a motivation to keep trips to a minimum.

dark green Get rid of your car: in Montreal on Car-free Day 2004, there was a 90 per cent drop in nitrogen monoxide and 100 per cent drop in carbon monoxide. This may be tricky in places without good public transport, and costly (fuel and motoring prices don't reflect environmental costs), but kids whose parents use alternatives to cars are likely to be less car-dependent, more active, and healthier.

ENVIRONMENTAL TOXINS

When you're out and about with your baby, reassure yourself that environmental pollutants can be many times less concentrated outdoors than inside the home.

In a traffic jam, **air pollution** is 3 times **higher in the car** than on the pavement

Each year, some 70,000 different chemicals are released into the environment, many by industry and farming. We are exposed to them wherever and however we live, and not only when we venture outdoors. They are in the air we breathe, the food we eat (or the toys we suck), the water we drink, and the consumer goods we choose. Babies are uniquely vulnerable to the effects of some chemicals in the atmosphere because their cell walls are more permeable than adults'; their nervous, immune, and reproductive systems are still developing; and their detox organs (the liver and kidneys) are not fully functioning.

Hormone-disrupting chemicals in the environment are worrying because they have the ability to scramble our hormone-regulating system. Even trace levels of the most toxic – known as POPs (persistent organic pollutants) – are harmful, especially to infants, and have been linked with reproductive, behavioural, and immunity problems, and cancer. They are found in everything from fire retardants in furniture and electronics to food, cosmetics, textile finishes, stain protectors, car interiors, non-stick pans, trainers, carpets, and clingfilm. Need a glass of water? Alongside hormone-disrupting chemicals, it might contain deadly heavy metals and nitrates that reduce the ability of haemoglobin in blood to carry oxygen. Take a deep breath, but not too deep; particulates from car exhausts and PAHs (polycyclic aromatic hydrocarbons, air pollutants created in combustion) from car and heating fumes and cigarette smoke, threaten city dwellers especially. But don't panic; exposure is a fact of modern life, and you can take steps to minimize the risks to your baby. Do get angry enough to write to your MP and join an environmental organization that campaigns on the issue.

How to reduce your baby's exposure

- Fit a water filter.
- Only use certified organic toiletries; your baby doesn't need any bodycare products until he's ready for toothpaste.
- Use eco washing and cleaning products.
- Walk, don't drive: air pollution is higher within a car than outside it during peak travel times.
- Eat organic and dress second-hand.
- Don't smoke: babies exposed to PAHs and smoke are more likely to have breathing problems and asthma diagnoses.

KEEPING SAFE IN THE SUN

A baby's skin is five times thinner than an adult's skin and doesn't yet have a fully developed outer protective layer, so make sure you keep your baby covered up in the sun.

The best cover-up is not a chemical sunscreen – even an organic formulation. Insufficient research has been done into the safety of long-term use of sun creams on young children (even though some nurseries won't accept children in summer unless they are wearing sunscreen). Probably the least worrying product is a sunblock, which usually contains ingredients such as zinc or titanium dioxide that sit on the skin's surface, deflecting harmful UV rays. These types of products usually tinge the skin white. Sunscreens are different because they are made from chemical "sponges" that absorb the sun's UV rays and penetrate the skin – and so don't turn it white. According to the US Environmental Working Group, most sunscreens contain suspect ingredients, such as hormone-disrupting parabens and PABA. If a sunblock or sunscreen boasts that it contains "nano" ingredients – tiny particles of chemicals – it's probably best to avoid it, since these molecules are so small they may be able to enter the bloodstream; the effects of this are unknown.

A wide-brimmed hat and cover-up clothing are a better choice than sunscreen. Choose lightweight clothes in natural, breathable fabrics with long sleeves or trousers. Hemp is a

Keep babies out of direct sunlight and dress them in light, long-sleeved tops, trousers, and a hat.

naturally UV-resistant fabric. As an extra precaution, fill your child's plate with sun-protective fruit and vegetables (they tend to be naturally red, orange, or yellow in colour). Use a sunshade on your buggy and plan outdoor play sessions for times when the sun is less strong: before 11am and after 4pm.

TRAVELLING FURTHER AFIELD

Plane journeys are the world's fastest growing source of CO_2 emissions – and also a nightmare with a wriggly baby on your lap. So what are the greener and easier options for getting away?

Counter-intuitively, planes tend to emit fewer greenhouse gases per person than cars – especially if you drive a gas-guzzling 4x4. And some journeys on a full, less polluting plane may be more carbon efficient than driving the same distance by car. The problem is that planes generally travel much greater distances than cars, magnifying the carbon emissions. One single transatlantic flight, for instance, uses more carbon than a whole year's driving in an average car. Planes also deposit warming agents (not just carbon dioxide, but nitrogen and vapour trails) into the atmosphere at high altitude, which may greatly increase their warming impact.

If you are planning to carbon off-set your journey (funding tree-planting or environmental projects in developing countries), do some research first. Companies offering the service are unregulated, the effects of their projects may be hard to verify, and, in the case of tree-planting, the environmental benefits are decades away. It may be better to reduce your emissions by insulating your loft, or to avoid them completely by not taking that flight. Greener alternatives to the plane are all pretty stressful with a baby or toddler. A train journey may be nine

When you pay for an off-set you're not actually neutralizing your carbon impact

times more carbon efficient than a plane trip, but is limited in terms of baby entertainment. Electric trains, such as France's TGV fleet, are the most carbon-light.

Long-distance buses can be a greener way to get places, especially if they run on biodiesel or hydrogen fuel cells. But hours of jiggling a restless baby and holding him to the window to take in the view can be tiresome. Ferries can be a more fun way to travel slowly: you can find crawling space and a high chair, endure a toddler play area or child entertainer, or perhaps even go for a swim. If you book a cabin, you can even keep to your baby's regular pattern of naps. However, some ferries emit  more carbon dioxide than planes, especially high-speed ferries.

The greenest plan is to travel less often. The average Briton who flies takes about six flights a year. Maybe it's time to rethink how frequently you take weekend breaks abroad or longhaul flights. Can you cut your quota to just one return trip? Having a baby makes you to reconsider every part of your life, so why not cast your net a little wider to include the whole planet?

Conclusion

Now you've started to change your own life to make it greener, why not spread the word to family, friends, and beyond? Having the support of others really helps to counter green fatigue.

What you can do

- Ask for wooden toys at gift-giving occasions.
- Spread the word that your baby only wears organic or Fairtrade clothing.
- Become a breastfeeding counsellor.
- Talk your child's playgroup or nursery into using eco cleaning products or switching to a green energy tariff – join the committee to influence which toys and food they buy.
- Involve everyone who looks after your child in your green lifestyle, from nannies to grannies.
- Teach younger family members the basics of home cooking.
- Throw a baby and toddler party in a local park and invite all the children in your street.

We can only make the world a **greener** place if we **act together**

Green resources

Campaigning organizations

www.cat.org.uk
Centre for Alternative Technology: Europe's leading eco centre; provides info on green electricity, biodiesel, and buying a new washing-machine.

www.foe.co.uk
Friends of the Earth: explore climate change and support campaigns.

www.greenpeace.org.uk
Greenpeace: join campaigns to defend habitats and eliminate toxic chemicals.

www.nct.org.uk
National Childbirth Trust: a charity offering information and support to parents.

www.soilassociation.org
Soil Association: organic accreditation body; information on food and pesticides.

www.ewg.org
US Environmental Working Group: exposes threats to health and the environment; how to take action.

www.wen.org.uk
Women's Environmental Network: info on real nappies, sanitary protection, and toxic cosmetics.

www.panda.org
WWF (World Wildlife Fund): fight "human-induced" change to the planet.

Child health

www.mailman.hs.columbia.edu/ccceh/pollution.html
Columbia Centre for Children's Environmental Health: research on the effects of pollution and contaminants.

www.healthychild.org
Healthy Child Healthy World (formerly CHEC): what's harmful for babies; tour a chemical-free home.

www.homeopathy-soh.org
Society of Homeopaths: find a homeopath and homeopathic pharmacy.

www.epa.gov
US Environmental Protection Agency: find out why chemicals in household cleaners can be harmful.

www.van.org.uk
Vaccine Awareness Network: details of the ingredients of childhood vaccines.

Energy-saving

www.cat.org.uk/carbongym
Carbon Gym: calculate the cost of your carbon habits; learn how to reduce them.

www.energysavingtrust.org.uk
Energy Saving Trust: simple ways to reduce your energy use at home.

Ethical consuming

www.actionaid.org.uk
Action Aid: the "Who Pays?" campaign highlights corporate accountability.

www.ejfoundation.org
Environmental Justice Campaign: find out about cotton production, illegal fishing, and child labour.

www.ethicalconsumer.org
Ethical Consumer Research Association: find an "ethiscore" for various products.

www.fsc.org
Forest Stewardship Council: certifies timber and "forest products" that protect forests and forest-dependent peoples.

www.freecycle.org
The Freecycle Network: global movement of "giving and getting stuff for free".

www.frn.org.uk
Furniture Reuse Network: where to donate your unwanted furniture and why.

www.globaltrees.org
National Directory of Reclaimed Furniture Suppliers: lists craftspeople making furniture in the UK using only reclaimed timber.

www.sofaproject.org.uk
Sofa Project: the UK's leading furniture and electrical appliance reuse charity.

www.waronwant.org
War on Want: information about the working practices behind cheap clothes.

Green baby goods

www.greenfibres.com
Greenfibres: eco baby goods, plus resources on eco-fibres and certification.

www.naturalcollection.com
Natural Collection: online eco department store.

www.realnappycampaign.com
The Real Nappy Campaign: call for the nearest source of cloth nappies.

www.naturalclothing.co.uk
Schmidt Natural Clothing: ethically sourced organic, biodynamic, and Fairtrade clothing and nappies.

www.beamingbaby.com
Beaming Baby: online store for baby products, offering retail and wholesale.

Green foods

www.abm.me.uk
Association of Breastfeeding Mothers: charity offering friendly support.

www.babyledweaning.com
Baby-led Weaning: how to skip puréed food and jump straight to family food.

www.breastfeedingnetwork.org.uk
The Breastfeeding Network: leaflets, support centres, and a helpline.

www.eattheseasons.co.uk
Eat the Seasons: what's fresh and delicious in Britain, month by month.

www.laleche.org.uk
La Leche League: mother-to-mother breastfeeding support and helpline.

www.mcsuk.org
Marine Conservation Society: find out which fish are better choices to eat.

www.farmersmarkets.net
National Farmer's Retail and Markets Association: find a local certified market.

Green toys

www.natll.org.uk
National Association of Toy and Leisure Libraries: read about the benefits and find your nearest.

www.toys-to-you.co.uk
Toys to You: affordable ethical toys and a toy recycling scheme.

www.holz-toys.co.uk
Holz Toys: environmentally sound, hand-crafted toys, many of which are wooden.

Greener travel

www.thebabywearer.com
The Baby Wearer: global reviews of slings and research into "baby-wearing".

www.carplus.org.uk
Carplus: click on a map to find out about your nearest car club.

www.worldcarfree.net
World Carfree Network: statistics and arguments for giving up your car.

Glossary

ACO: Australian Certified Organic.

Antioxidants: molecules that minimize the harmful effects of free radicals, typically found in certain fruit and vegetables.

BDIH: the Federation of German Industries and Trading certifies natural cosmetics as not tested on animals and GM-free; manufacture is eco-friendly.

CE Marking: safety mark certifying the product's conformity to the essential requirements of European law.

Dioxins: dangerous toxins, formed as byproducts of certain manufacturing processes; some are known carcinogens.

Fairtrade: the Fairtrade mark is an independent consumer label which guarantees producers in the developing world are getting a better deal.

Flavonoids: a group of compounds with antioxidant properties (also known as bioflavonoids).

FSC: the Forest Stewardship Council, promotes responsible management of the world's forests.

GM: genetically modified crops or organisms have been altered artificially to produce desirable characteristics.

KRAV: the Swedish body regulating organic standards belongs to the International Federation of Organic Agriculture Movements.

Lion Mark: a consumer safety symbol.

Nonylphenol: a man-made organic compound, used as an industrial surfactant, but now banned in the EU.

Organotins: tin-based compounds, used industrially as heat stabilizers and as biocides, but highly toxic to marine life.

PABA: para-aminobenzoic acid, used as a filter in sunscreens, but linked to cancer.

PAHs: polycyclic aromatic hydrocarbons, released in combustion, are associated with many dangers to health.

PCBs: polychlorinated biphenyls had various industrial uses, but are now banned and classed as POPs.

Phthalates: compounds used mainly as plasticizers, linked to hormone disruption.
  BBP: butyl benzyl phthalate.
  DBP: di-n-butyl phthalate.
  DEHP: di (2-ethylhexyl) phthalate.
  DIDP: di-isodecyl phthalate.
  DINP: di-isononyl phthalate.
  DNOP: di-n-octyl phthalate.

POPs: persistent organic pollutants.

PVC: polyvinyl chloride is a plastic with very many commercial applications; it is thought to pose significant health risks.

SLS: sodium lauryl sulphate is a surfactant detergent; it is found in the majority of bodycare products, and is associated with various health complaints.

Toluene: a water-insoluble liquid used in industrial products; chronic inhalation can result in brain damage.

US EPA: United States Environmental Protection Agency.

UV: ultraviolet electromagnetic radiation.

VOCs: volatile organic compounds.

Index

Acknowledgments

Author's acknowledgments
The author would like to thank: Ethical Consumer; CAT; Weleda; Greg and Teresa Pascoe at Cusgarne Farm; Paul Slydel at Cycle Solutions (01326 377003); Julia Linfoot BSc MCPH RSHom for text on homeopathic remedies; toxicologist John Marriott; Mary Mathieson; and everyone at DK, especially Penny and Peggy, and above all Tara and Hannah.

Publisher's acknowledgments
Dorling Kindersley would like to thank Sue Bosanko for indexing; Alyson Silverwood for proofreading; Peggy Sadler for design assistance; Andrea Bagg and Diana Vowles for editorial assistance; the following for the loan of props: Yummies (01273 738733), Great Expectations (01273 622993), Greenfibres, Holz Toys, Beaming Baby, Wool Shed (www. woolshed.co.uk), Little Hooligan (www. littlehooligan.com), Bamboo Baby (www. bamboobaby.co.uk), Tatty Bumpkin (www. tattybumpkin.com), By Nature (www. bynature.co.uk), Blackout Kitsch (01273 671741), Hen & Hammock (www. henandhammock.co.uk), Sidney Street Bikes, and Paperpod (www.paperpod.co.uk). Our models were: Miro & Mina Lloyd, Eleanor & Isabella Moore–Smith, Kitty & Juliette Kinsman, Sarah Coats & Rafael Apey, Louise Rainey & Samuel Pole, Jeya James, Amias Limerick, Elizabeth Apple & Isla Apple Hall, Corrine Ashgar, Oliver & Alex Roberts, Ry Zeferino–Birchall, Amber Asamoa, Ruby Baker, Torsten Van Ande, Meera Vithaldas, Gaia Dean & Mia Beugre, Heather Lewis & Robyn Moody, Nicole Drysdale, John, Ruben & Louis Harrison, Hannah Bellanche, Mattie Barrett, Kevin Smith, Rachael Parfitt & Eddie Hunt